# Learning to Live

# from the Acts

*Books by Eugenia Price . . .*

Fiction
  THE BELOVED INVADER
  NEW MOON RISING
Nonfiction
  DISCOVERIES
  THE BURDEN IS LIGHT
  NEVER A DULL MOMENT
  EARLY WILL I SEEK THEE
  SHARE MY PLEASANT STONES
  WOMAN TO WOMAN
  WHAT IS GOD LIKE?
  BELOVED WORLD
  A WOMAN'S CHOICE
  FIND OUT FOR YOURSELF
  GOD SPEAKS TO WOMEN TODAY
  THE WIDER PLACE
  MAKE LOVE YOUR AIM
  JUST AS I AM
  LEARNING TO LIVE FROM THE GOSPELS
  THE UNIQUE WORLD OF WOMEN

# Learning To Live From The Acts

*by*

# Eugenia Price

TURNER

PUBLISHING COMPANY

Turner Publishing Company
Nashville, Tennessee
www.turnerpublishing.com

Cover design: Bruce Gore

Library of Congress Cataloging-in-Publication Data Upon Request

9781684427154  paperback
9781684427161  hardback
9781684427178  ebook

# 🜍 PREFACE

Even in our technological era, there is no way to cope with the content of the book called the Acts of the Apostles if the reader rejects the fact that there is a living, energetically active Holy Spirit. The men and women written about in this lively New Testament book simply could not have acted as they did on their own. Something happened to them on the Day of Pentecost that turned them and their world upside down by pragmatic standards. Grieving, nervous, discouraged men who had, only days before, been hiding in a locked room, afraid for their lives, moved at once out into the streets of Jerusalem, full of courage, balance, spirit— their sorrowing at an end, life suddenly worth living,

Consider their grief by itself for a moment. The Man whom they had loved and trusted enough to desert their families and their jobs to follow, the Master in whom they believed as children believe in a good father, their

King who was going to re-establish the throne of David
and put them all in important positions in it was gone—
crucified like a criminal between two thieves. Their
hopes for their own futures lay in the blood and the
dust at the foot of that now empty cross; but, more important than that, their dearest Friend was dead.

How, then, could some concentrated kind of psycho-
logical phenomenon on the Day of the Jewish Feast
of Pentecost have caused those grieving, broken hearts
to mend in a matter of minutes? If God had not kept
his word given to them through Jesus to send a Comforter—the Holy Spirit—how did they become the
men and women whose grief ended suddenly and never
returned? This is not the way of grief for human beings.
Real grief seldom ends. The healthy mind, fixed on
God, can learn to live with it, but not instantly. It often
takes years.

The men and women who entered the Upper Room
to wait "in one accord" for the promised Comforter
were wearing the same clothes when they poured out
into the streets on Pentecost; they looked the same
physically, but they were not the same. They had heard
no sermons on how to handle grief and fear; they had
read no books; they had merely waited together until
the One whom they loved and believed in—and
mourned—came back to them! The dear, familiar
voice was still; the loved, familiar figure no longer
walked up ahead, leading them—but in a way only
God can explain, their Master was suddenly back. Back,
living his life in the person of the Holy Spirit—not
with them, as he had been before, but *in* them: in their

very bodies and minds and hearts. They were no longer on their own. The very Spirit of the God who created them and redeemed them in Jesus Christ was available to these simple people as Jesus had never been available to them. When he had walked the dusty roads and climbed the barren hills with them during their three years together, he had taught and inspired and encouraged them, but then he had had no means of energizing them from within, no way to enlighten their minds from within, no way to strengthen their hearts. Now, suddenly, he could, and the riotous, joy-filled, sometimes tragic, but always triumphant story of the early Church began to "happen."

The Acts of the Apostles is not a complete biography of Paul or even a partial one, although a generous part of the adventure is Paul's. Neither is it Peter's story, or Stephen's, or Barnabas', or John's. It is as though the writer, Luke, felt it quite sufficient merely to give us a glimpse of the continuing difference it made in each life, detailed enough and covering just enough time to make it perfectly clear that these things can go on happening—that life can go on being this way for anyone who follows Jesus Christ and obeys the promptings of his Spirit within. The short account is uneven, minutely descriptive in parts, swift and merely outlined in others. Rather than writing a carefully planned treatise, Luke has seemed to flash a bright light on what he felt should be an example of the daily lives of all believers in the risen Lord he followed. Here and there in the first conflict-torn, joy-filled days of the early Church, we are permitted to see for ourselves how it was meant to be for us who call ourselves Christians.

Why it is not this way for us now, or why it is, at best, only this way now and then, I feel we must decide. I find little or no doctrine in the Acts, but I do find life, and great and simple helps in learning to live it.

The people whose lives we glimpse in these pages were not spiritual giants—not even Paul. They were just people with personality and disposition defects like our own, with needs and problems and weaknesses we can all recognize. Even Paul did not eventually become a perfect man—no one did. No one does. But they all *grew* if they obeyed the promptings of the very real, living Spirit within them. I once heard a young lady exclaim: "Well, if those people in that group at our church are filled with the Holy Spirit and are still as unattractive as they are, I don't want to be!" An older, wiser man smiled at her and replied: "But, my dear, just think how repulsive they must have been without Him!"

I thought of this little true story as I worked through the Acts of the Apostles and rejoiced that God didn't have to limit himself to spiritually superior people. There aren't any, really, and so we are the ones who are blessed, because he limited himself to us and then figured out a way through the Holy Spirit to make our potentials limitless.

EUGENIA PRICE

St. Simons Island, Georgia
February, 1970

# The Acts of the Apostles

 CHAPTER 1

vv. 1 and 2

*The former treatise have I made, O Theophilus, of all that Jesus began both to do and teach, Until the day in which he was taken up, after that he through the Holy Ghost had given commandments unto the apostles whom he had chosen:*

Most authorities agree that Luke had not yet completed certain portions of his Gospel, but at least he had written enough to be convinced that, as always, Jesus was taking every precaution to be sure His followers understood at least something of the strange events of the past days. Until the day of his return to the Father, Jesus patiently instructed them. He has not changed.

v. 3

*To whom also he shewed himself alive after his passion by many infallible proofs, being seen of them forty days, and speaking of the things pertaining to the kingdom of God:*

The Master was not only infinitely careful with his chosen ones, mindful that they were not yet filled with

the Spirit; he stayed on earth in his resurrected body
for forty days, giving them "many infallible proofs"
that his Resurrection was a true resurrection—not a
theory, not a rumor. The Biblical account does not tell
us about everyone he visited during these forty days,
but it does say that he was "seen of them forty days."
He must have covered a lot of ground, must have spent
the entire forty days making certain that none of his
own doubted that the Father *had* literally brought
him from the grave. And daily he kept talking to them
about the true kingdom of God—as always, doing all
he could to protect them from confusion.

v. 4

*And, being assembled together with them, com-
manded them that they should not depart from Jerusalem, but wait for the promise of the Father, which,
saith he, ye have heard of me.*

At this particular meeting, Jesus gave them the central instruction, the specific commandment: They were
not to leave Jerusalem, but wait for the Father's promise. His Father had never let Jesus down, even when
he was on the cross. There was to be no questioning
of the promise now. Their problem would be waiting.
Our timing is seldom on schedule with God's, but
waiting can be a far stronger faith-builder than quickly
answered prayer.

v. 5

*For John truly baptized with water; but ye shall be baptized with the Holy Ghost not many days hence.*

Even now, Jesus did not minimize the work of John the Baptist. This is a stunning example of God's willingness to enter into the limitations of time with us. Living in the *eternal now* as he does, he was (and is) still acting in the concept of time which human beings can understand. First, John the Baptist, who "truly baptized with water." Now the next step was coming: In a few days, these people who believed were going to be baptized with the Holy Spirit. God does not need to do one thing and then the next for us in that time-bound sequence—like a ribbon stretched out—except for our sakes. And we are still his first concern.

v. 6

*When they therefore were come together, they asked of him, saying, Lord, wilt thou at this time restore again the kingdom to Israel?*

They simply did not understand and could not be expected to understand. Their understanding would be opened only *after* the Holy Spirit entered their very lives. Like many of us, they asked a stupid question— a superficial question—a self-centered, self-seeking question—a human question. Their concern was still not outward, but inward. How will all this help those of us who are Israelites? they asked.

v. 7

*And he said unto them, It is not for you to know the times or the seasons, which the Father hath put in his own power.*

This was not a divine "put-down." Jesus is simply helping them get a perspective.

v. 8

*. . . ye shall receive power . . . and ye shall be witnesses unto me. . . .*

If we miss this, we miss everything. No one is to seek "power from on high" in order to experience a spiritual excitement, or to perform miracles, or to be considered "advanced in the things of God." We are to receive power for only one purpose: to be witnesses unto Jesus Christ himself. Not to the organized Church or to our own holiness, but to Christ.

vv. 9 through 14

*And when he had spoken these things . . . he was taken up . . . out of their sight. And while they looked . . . two men stood by them in white apparel; Which also said, Ye men of Galilee, why stand ye gazing up into heaven? this same Jesus . . . shall so come in like manner as ye have seen him go. . . . Then returned they unto Jerusalem . . . went up into an upper room, [and] continued with one accord in prayer and supplication. . . .*

At the moment Jesus disappeared out of their sight, God caused them to see two Messengers who, for that moment, told them all they needed to know. The result? They did as Jesus had instructed. Peter and James and John and Andrew and Philip and Thomas and Bartholomew and Matthew and James the son of Alpheus and Simon the zealot and James' brother, Judas, along with the faithful women and Mary, Jesus' mother, and his brothers, began the waiting time. Suddenly they could wait. Their questions were stilled. One hundred and twenty people of one mind makes for quiet.

vv. 24a and 26a (Read vv. 15 through 26.)

*And they prayed. . . . And they gave forth their lots; and the lot fell upon Matthias. . . .*

As with the little girl who "prayed and crossed her fingers," the disciples mixed faith with expediency here. The Holy Spirit had not yet come, and so we can't blame them for using their wits instead of waiting for guidance from God. Peter evidently grew impatient and decided that he might as well get some business transacted while they waited, so he prayed and then instructed his brothers to cast lots to determine who among them would take Judas' place. Matthias must have been well liked—they had nominated him for the position. He was undoubtedly loyal, but evidently he was not God's choice. Their waiting was faulty. God, as he always does, did the best he could with Matthias until his own choice was made in Paul some months later.

 CHAPTER 2

v. 1

> *And when the day of Pentecost was fully come, they were all with one accord in one place.*

Though still powerless, except for the use of human devices, at least the one hundred and twenty were *there* where Jesus had told them to be and they were "with one accord." Their faith, sincere as it surely was, had reached out to act in the choosing of the twelfth disciple, but it had acted on merely human wisdom. The promised power had not yet come. They were doing their best, but their best had never been enough. It could not be expected to be enough now. Nine long days and nights had dragged by, but the followers of Christ were still acting on a strictly human level. Their "chosen committee" was in session, but only human power was available.

vv. 2 through 5

> *And suddenly there came a sound from heaven as of a rushing mighty wind, and it filled all the house where they were sitting. And there appeared unto them cloven tongues like as of fire, and it sat upon each of them.*

*And they were all filled with the Holy Ghost, and began to speak with other tongues, as the Spirit gave them utterance. And there were dwelling at Jerusalem Jews, devout men, out of every nation under heaven.*

Jerusalem was thronging with visitors on the Jewish Feast of Pentecost, and when the sudden wind struck the Holy City a little before nine, the narrow streets were crowded with terrified, jostling people, crowding, elbowing their way into shops and inns—anywhere to escape the blowing dust and debris. In Jerusalem that day were Partians, Medes, Elamites, Mesopotamians, Judeans, Cappadocians, travelers from Pontus, Asia, Phrygia, Pamphylia, Egypt, Cyrene, Rome, Crete and Arabia. Almost every known language was represented that day. When people from the same locales met, crowding into any kind of shelter against the driving wind, they lapsed into their own native tongues.

There was no darkness, no rain—only the great roaring from heaven as the people stared into the now empty streets in wonder at what was happening. Suddenly the wind stopped, and before the confused visitors to Jerusalem began to pour back into the streets, down the narrow stair from the upper room where the one hundred and twenty had waited, the disciples of Jesus came, praising God and clapping their hands with joy—shouting their praises in tongues familiar to every visitor in the city. They were not speaking in *unknown tongues*. They spoke in tongues *known* to all of Jerusalem's visitors.

vv. 6 through 8

*Now when this was noised abroad, the multitude came together, and were confounded, because that every man heard them speak in his own language. And they were all amazed and marvelled, saying one to another, Behold, are not all these which speak Galilaeans? And how hear we every man in our own tongue, wherein we were born?*

In the land of disciples were housewives, seamstresses, farmers, fishermen, carpenters—not an intellectual among them—all Galileans who, as everyone knew, spoke colloquial Aramaic. How could this odd assortment of country folk suddenly begin to speak intelligently and plainly in every language known to man? And how was it that what they said was all in praise of the living God?

vv. 12, 13

*And they were all amazed, and were in doubt, saying one to another, What meaneth this? Others mocking said, These men are full of new wine.*

The glib explanation of this strange, surprising behavior of the disciples is most understandable, especially among those who turn first, in any emotional emergency, to scorn. When in doubt, just say "They're drunk!" The disciples *were* full of a "new wine"—the wine of the Kingdom of God, the very life of God Himself in the person of his Holy Spirit.

v. 14

*But Peter, standing up with the eleven, lifted up his voice, and said unto them . . .*

Peter did not take over on his own and do the deciding this time. He stood up "with the eleven." His very life had been invaded by the life of God, and he could now both lean on and support his brothers, with far less thought for his own prestige.

vv. 29 through 32 (Read vv. 15 through 28.)

*Men and brethren, let me freely speak unto you of the patriarch David, that he is both dead and buried, and his sepulchre is with us unto this day. Therefore being a prophet, and knowing that God had sworn with an oath to him, that of the fruit of his loins, according to the flesh, he would raise up Christ to sit on his throne; He seeing this before spake of the resurrection of Christ, that his soul was not left in hell, neither his flesh did see corruption. This Jesus hath God raised up, whereof we all are witnesses.*

Now Peter saw it all as he had never been able to see before. And as he preached his first sermon in the power of the Holy Spirit on the streets of Jerusalem that day, he bore down on dead center—Jesus had risen from the dead! His body had not been stolen and hidden from sight to make it seem as though he had been resurrected from the dead; *he had gotten up* and walked out of that tomb and, at the very moment Peter spoke, was alive in the presence of the Father. And

Peter was being obedient to this living Lord by witnessing—not unto his own "emotional high" of the moment, not unto the spiritual thrill of speaking in a tongue he had never used before, but unto "this Jesus" whom God had "raised up."

vv. 40 and 41

*And with many other words did he testify and exhort, saying, Save yourselves from this untoward generation. Then they that gladly received his word were baptized: and the same day there were added unto them about three thousand souls.*

From one hundred and twenty, their number jumped to three thousand, one hundred and twenty— all because Peter spoke on the one essential, the bodily resurrection from the dead of Jesus Christ. Daily more continued to be added to their number, and "many wonders and signs were done by the apostles. And all that believed were together, and had all things common." Harmony and peace were there among them because they were united around the *single event in history* powerful enough to make them one: This Jesus had been God himself visiting their earth, and now his Spirit lived within them. He was no longer gone. He was back. They could stop grieving. Their Master could help them now, strengthen them from within, as even he had not been able to do when he walked with them as a Man. There among these simple people was a bond which had come *not* because they had "spoken in tongues" together—this had been done by God simply so that those still in darkness in Jerusalem that day could understand. They were not one because of a shared emotional ecstasy. These people were one because at this point in their young church life together they were still on center—Jesus Christ was still their Lord. They "had favor with all the people" because Christ lived in them. He was, as he had said, drawing people to himself because he was being "lifted up." It takes no profound thinker to discover what is missing today.

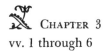 CHAPTER 3

vv. 1 through 6

*Now Peter and John went up together into the temple at the hour of prayer. . . . And a certain man lame from his mother's womb was carried, whom they laid daily at the gate of the temple which is called Beautiful, to ask alms of them that entered into the temple; Who seeing Peter and John about to go into the temple asked an alms. And Peter, fastening his eyes upon him with John, said, Look on us. And he gave heed unto them, expecting to receive something of them. Then Peter said, Silver and gold have I none; but such as I have give I thee: In the name of Jesus Christ of Nazareth rise up and walk.*

Peter had lost his shyness. The very life of God was in him, and that left no more need for denials, for slinking away by night pretending that he did not know Jesus. Peter had lost his need for wasted motion. He could now go straight to the point without fear, without hedging, with the inner strength of the Master himself.

v. 7

*And he took him by the right hand, and lifted him up: and immediately his feet and ankle bones received strength.*

Peter did not think of pleading with God to heal this man. He expected it to happen. The years had not dimmed his memory of the Master's touch on crippled legs. Without a single course at the seminary, Peter had the sure knowledge that the same power had now come to indwell his own being.

vv. 8 and 9

*And he leaping up stood, and walked, and entered with them into the temple, walking, and leaping, and praising God. And all the people saw him walking and praising God:*

It is our *walk* that people watch.

vv. 11 and 12

*And as the lame man which was healed held Peter and John, all the people ran together unto them in the porch that is called Solomon's, greatly wondering. And when Peter saw it, he answered unto the people, Ye men of Israel, why marvel ye at this? or why look ye so earnestly on us, as though by our own power or holiness we had made this man to walk?*

Peter had already begun to make use of every opportunity to turn the people's attention to Jesus.

vv. 13 through 15

*The God of Abraham, and of Isaac, and of Jacob, the God of our fathers, hath glorified his Son Jesus; whom ye delivered up, and denied him in the presence of Pilate, when he was determined to let him go. But ye denied the Holy One and the Just, and desired a murderer to be granted unto you; And killed the Prince of life, whom God hath raised from the dead; whereof we are witnesses.*

Peter spoke directly to the central issue. "Ye are to be witnesses unto me." Not unto a healing—unto *me*.

v. 17

*[But] now, brethren, I wot that through ignorance ye did it, as did also your rulers.*

Peter had really been changed! It had always been his nature to jump to conclusions. He was balanced now that the Spirit of the God of balance lived in him. He showed clearly not merely the kindness of God, but God's very understanding of people. He was not thumping a pulpit, shouting accusations at the men who listened to him that day. He pointed no fingers, screaming that they would all be damned in their sins. He began by calling them "brothers"—no hint of spiritual superiority. These people who stood hearing Peter did not agree with him yet, but he called them his brothers. As his Master had always done, Peter was reaching toward them with an open hand. And then, he showed God's understanding. Quite simply, he told them he realized that they had "killed the Prince of life" out of ignorance of who He was. Peter even included the silk-robed Pharisees and rulers in his sweeping invitation to forgiveness. He had heard this done before. He had heard John tell of the familiar voice crying out: "Father, forgive them; for they know not what they do." The same Spirit lived in Peter now and in John. They could be open, receptive, welcoming, understanding. They could be as gentle as they were strong in the power of the crucified and risen Lord they loved.

### CHAPTER 4
vv. 1 through 4

*And as they spake unto the people, the priests, and the captain of the temple, and the Sadducees, came upon them, Being grieved that they taught the people, and preached through Jesus the resurrection from the dead. And they laid hands on them, and put them in hold unto the next day: for it was now eventide. Howbeit many of them which heard the word believed; and the number of the men was about five thousand.*

Suddenly it was all right with Peter and John to be thrown in prison. The fear that had driven them both to desert Jesus on the dark night of his crucifixion had been pushed out by the entrance of the same Spirit that kept their Master strong and unafraid. It was of very fleeting importance to them now that they were tossed into jail for the night. The important thing had taken place: Five thousand new believers had been added to their number. They could rejoice over that in jail as well as they could have at home.

vv. 5 through 8

*And it came to pass on the morrow, that their rulers, and elders, and scribes, And Annas the high priest, and Caiaphas, and John, and Alexander, and as many as were of the kindred of the high priest, were gathered together at Jerusalem. And when they had set them in the midst, they asked, By what power, or by what name, have ye done this? Then Peter, filled with the Holy Ghost, said unto them . . .*

The important fact here was not what might happen to Peter and John before this mighty array of rulers who would decide their punishment; the thing that mattered was that here was another unexpected opportunity for Peter to preach a sermon about Jesus Christ. And preach it he did (verses 9 through 12).

v. 13

*Now when they saw the boldness of Peter and John, and perceived that they were unlearned and ignorant men, they marvelled; and they took knowledge of them, that they had been with Jesus.*

Peter and John had accomplished the ultimate: showing, even to their enemies, that "they had been with Jesus."

v. 14

*And beholding the man which was healed standing with them, they could say nothing against it.*

The rulers sent Peter and John outside while they conferred, but there stood the man who had been healed —what could even they say against a thing like that? Oh, the two disciples were warned never to speak in the name of Jesus again, but Peter and John had been given the holy boldness of God along with his spirit, and they merely went back to the other disciples and prayed for still more courage to speak the truth.

vv. 31 and 32

*And when they had prayed, the place was shaken where they were assembled together; and they were all filled with the Holy Ghost, and they spake the word of God with boldness. And the multitude of them that believed were of one heart and of one soul: neither said any of them that ought of the things which he possessed was his own; but they had all things common.*

With the prayer to speak the truth with boldness even in the face of imprisonment and flogging, there came to the band of believers a new kind of naturalness together. There is no record that anyone laid down the law about communal living, but suddenly, with that fresh visitation of the Spirit, all personal possessiveness came to an abrupt end: ". . . neither said any of them that ought of the things which he possessed was his own." Now, this is *not* natural with man, but it brought a new *naturalness* among them: the *naturalness* of the Kingdom of God. If God is love, then it is his very nature to love. If this nature indwells us by the Holy Spirit, then it becomes natural for us to love. Love does not possess. Love gives. The disciples began to live by *giving love.*

v. 37

*Having land, [they] sold it, and brought the money, and laid it at the apostles' feet.*

Again, there seem to have been no rules laid down. This act was spontaneous. Love had happened to them.

CHAPTER 5

vv. 1 through 5

*But a certain man named Ananias, with Sapphira his wife, sold a possession, And kept back part of the price, his wife also being privy to it, and brought a certain part, and laid it at the apostles' feet. But Peter said, Ananias, why hath Satan filled thine heart to lie to the Holy Ghost, and to keep back part of the price of the land? Whiles it remained, was it not thine own? and after it was sold, was it not in thine own power? why hast thou conceived this thing in thine heart? thou hast not lied unto men, but unto God. And Ananias hearing*

*these words fell down, and gave up the ghost: and great*
*fear came on all them that heard these things.*

I would be utterly presumptuous if I attempted an
explanation of why Ananias (and later, in verse 10, his
wife, Sapphira) dropped dead after their acts of trickery.
I do not believe that God arbitrarily kills those who
disobey him. If he did, none of us would be alive today.
If he acted in this way, think how short Jacob's life
would have been! I see nothing arbitrary in the nature
of Jesus Christ, and a Christian forms his concept of
God by Jesus. The only explanation of the sudden
deaths of this deceitful couple which has any meaning
for me is that the atmosphere in this first Christian community was so rarefied, so pure in love, that deceit in
the heart of anyone literally stopped that heart. If we
believe that Jesus was right when he said "the Kingdom is within," this is an acceptable explanation, although it may be partial. Actually, beyond normal
curiosity, I need no explanation of the deaths. I am
willing, as with so many passages from Scripture, to
wait until I am mature enough in Christ to comprehend more fully. For now, what I do understand of this
dramatic incident is quite enough to think about.
Whether it was actually Peter's duty or whether he was
being impulsive when he accused Ananias and his wife
is a moot question. But what strikes me is this: "thou
hast not lied unto men, but unto God." Peter may
have been taking things into his own hands by con-
demning Ananias and Sapphira, but what he said gives

me pause. I may get by with fooling you, but God's understanding of why I even tried to fool you is so complete that it might knock me dead if I glimpsed even a part of it.

At the end of verse 5, there is another stopper: "and great fear came on all them. . . ." Up to then, perfect love had kept away fear. The believers enjoyed their new life. Now, suddenly, they were afraid. The community structure had been weakened.

v. 14

*And believers were the more added to the Lord, multitudes both of men and women.*

For a brief time, love reigned, and then fear, and this is the last mention in the Acts of this communal life of sharing. What happened did not stop God, though—as our fears and prejudices and irregularities do not stop him now. We may slow him down, cause him to have to seek other channels through which to work, but he is God. He will remain in motion toward his children. "Believers *were* . . . added" anyway.

v. 24 (Read vv. 15 through 23.)

*Now when the high priest and the captain of the temple and the chief priests heard these things, they doubted of them whereunto this would grow.*

The last word in this verse is the key: *grow.* I am reminded by name of certain politicians who tremble as they look about them *seeing* the redefinition of freedom abroad in the world. *Seeing* some of us who have always been free joining forces with those who have been crippled by bondage. *Seeing* their precious political bases shake and crumble. *Seeing* love begin to *grow* across the world. God still permits his people to go to prison, but he also still knows how to open those doors which have been "shut with all safety."

vv. 25 through 28

*Then came one and told them, saying, Behold, the men whom ye put in prison are standing in the temple, and teaching the people. Then went the captain with the officers, and brought them without violence: for they feared the people, lest they should have been stoned. And when they had brought them, they set them before the council: and the high priest asked them, Saying, Did not we straitly command you that ye should not teach in this name? and, behold, ye have filled Jerusalem with your doctrine, and intend to bring this man's blood upon us.*

The account of the Acts of the Apostles is stunningly contemporary. Think back through the years since the school desegregation decision in 1954 by the United States Supreme Court. Like the early Christians, once fear and violence shattered their perfect communion twentieth-century apostles of equality and love have made mistakes; but prison doors still swing open, and the "captains of the temple" still rage when the courageous men and women walk the streets again preaching brotherhood and love.

vv. 29 through 33

*Then Peter and the other apostles answered and said, We ought to obey God rather than men. The God of our fathers raised up Jesus, whom ye slew and hanged on a tree. Him hath God exalted with his right hand to be a Prince and a Saviour, for to give repentance to Israel, and forgiveness of sins. And we are his witnesses of these things; and so is also the Holy Ghost, whom God hath given to them that obey him. When they heard that, they were cut to the heart, and took counsel to slay them.*

It is a painful thing to me that so many persons in the twentieth century who call themselves Christians do not believe that we "ought to obey God rather than man" when injustice is involved. I do not refer to the actions of violence-prone militants. I refer to such authentic exponents of Christian love and nonviolence as the late Martin Luther King, who spoke and acted as did Peter and the early apostles. And yet I have heard hundreds of contemporary Christians condemn Dr. King for civil disobedience. Peter thought of it first. Ultimately they killed him too.

vv. 34, 38 and 39

*Then stood there up one in the council, a Pharisee, named Gamaliel, a doctor of the law, had in reputation among all the people, and commanded to put the apostles forth a little space. . . . And now I say unto you, Refrain from these men, and let them alone: for if this counsel or this work be of men, it will come to nought:*

*But if it be of God, ye cannot overthrow it; lest haply ye be found even to fight against God.*

We can be thankful for the Gamaliels today, who choose to act by their innate wisdom and not by their emotions or their prejudices or their political prospects. They may not all be believers in Christ, as Gamaliel was not, but God can use them to keep love moving.

vv. 40 through 42

*And to him [Gamaliel] they agreed: and when they had called the apostles, and beaten them, they commanded that they should not speak in the name of Jesus, and let them go. And they departed from the presence of the council, rejoicing that they were counted worthy to suffer shame for his name. And daily in the temple, and in every house, they ceased not to teach and preach Jesus Christ.*

When men believe they are in God's will, even when they are afraid, they cannot be stopped. Their work will go on, and so will their rejoicing. Shame becomes glory.

 CHAPTER 6

vv. 1 through 3 and 5a

*And in those days, when the number of the disciples was multiplied, there arose a murmuring of the Grecians against the Hebrews, because their widows were neglected in the daily ministration. Then the twelve called the multitude of the disciples unto them, and said, It is not reason that we should leave the word of God, and serve tables. Wherefore, brethren, look ye out among you seven men of honest report, full of the Holy Ghost and wisdom, whom we may appoint over this business. . . . And the saying pleased the whole multitude: and they chose Stephen. . . .*

They chose six other worthy men too, but Stephen was the one of the seven so filled with God that, while he ministered fully to the widows and the poor, he could not be confined to menial work. This is no indictment of humble service—Stephen had been chosen to serve tables—but his spirit and his faith overflowed his appointed task. We should note here, also, that this is the first committee meeting of the organized Church. The Greeks among the Christian believers felt slighted. Something had to be done, so the brothers called a meeting and made appointments. As long as there is a Stephen appointed now and then, the organized Church will live, because Stephen, "full of faith and power, did great wonders and miracles among the people." He was not just a worthy servant; he resembled his Master.

v. 9

*Then there arose certain of the synagogue . . . disputing with Stephen.*

It never fails. Stephen was "living God" among them, and they couldn't bear it. The confrontation was too direct.

vv. 10 through 15

*And they were not able to resist the wisdom and the spirit by which he spake. Then they suborned [secretly incited] men, which said, We have heard him speak blasphemous words against Moses, and against God. And they stirred up the people, and the elders, and the scribes, and came upon him, and caught him, and brought him to the council. And set up false witnesses. . . . And all that sat in the council, looking stedfastly on him, saw his face as it had been the face of an angel.*

Stephen's persecutors managed to get some men to bear false witness against him. Stephen was called on the carpet before the self-righteous of the temple and accused of blasphemy—as his Saviour had been accused of it. What did Stephen do? He stood there with an expression on his face that made even these men think of an angel. Apparently, Stephen felt no need to say anything in his own defense. He just looked like Jesus.

 CHAPTER 7

v. 1 (Read vv. 2 through 54.)

*Then said the high priest, Are these things so?*

The whole of Chapter 7 has been called Stephen's defense. I do not see it as a defense. When the high priest asked him to speak, he did—eloquently, in marvelous order, covering Jewish history and the coming of the Messiah skillfully, clearly until his words so accused his accusers that they began to gnash their teeth in fury. One young intellectual named Saul of Tarsus stood back from the others as they rushed at Stephen, but his face was distorted with anger against the disciple.

vv. 55 and 56

*But he [Stephen], being full of the Holy Ghost, looked up stedfastly into heaven, and saw the glory of God, and Jesus standing on the right hand of God, And said, Behold, I see the heavens opened, and the Son of man standing on the right hand of God.*

Stephen did not see the angry mob rushing toward him with stones in their hands. He did not see Saul's hatred. Stephen was seeing, perhaps for the first time, that this Jesus whom he loved was more than merely the Jewish Messiah. He saw him as the Son of man— the Saviour of all men, universal, triumphant, "standing on the right hand of God." Jesus was not sitting down. He was *standing*, cheering Stephen on to act, even unto the moment of brutal death, in love. No wonder Stephen felt secure.

v. 57

*Then they cried out with a loud voice, and stopped their ears, and ran upon him with one accord.*

Why did they "stop their ears"? If I were in the process of stoning a man to death, I wouldn't want to hear his voice praising God either.

vv. 58 through 60

*[They] cast him out of the city, and stoned him: and the witnesses laid down their clothes at a young man's feet, whose name was Saul. And they stoned Stephen, [he] calling upon God, and saying, Lord Jesus, receive my spirit. And he kneeled down, and cried with a loud voice, Lord, lay not this sin to their charge. And when he had said this, he fell asleep.*

The young man, Saul of Tarsus, would find out for himself in a short time that Stephen was able to die forgiving his murderers, because *in Stephen* lived the same Spirit as in Christ. Stephen was filled with the Holy Spirit—the very Spirit of Jesus, whom he followed, the Spirit who never contradicts himself. Christ in Stephen would act no differently under the barrage of stones and curses than he had acted on the cross.

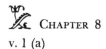 CHAPTER 8

v. 1 (a)

*And Saul was consenting unto his death.*

This short, dramatic verse ends Chapter 7 in most of the newer translations. Wherever it is placed, I feel guilt well up within me when I read it. Saul stood by and held the coats of those who threw the stones; but like us when we stand by and do nothing but hate, he was a murderer too.

vv. 1 (b) through 4

*And at that time there was a great persecution against the church which was at Jerusalem; and they were all scattered abroad throughout the regions of Judaea and Samaria, except the apostles. And devout men carried Stephen to his burial, and made great lamentation over him. As for Saul, he made havock of the church, entering into every house, and haling men and women committed them to prison. Therefore they that were scattered abroad went every where preaching the word.*

The same Spirit was living in the believers who were scattered by the persecutions. They "went every where preaching the word." What is eternally alive cannot be killed. Saul had watched Stephen die as Christ had died —praying for the forgiveness of his enemies. It incensed the young man, Saul, Gamaliel's student, and his hatred of the followers of the Crucified drove him to a special, scalding persecution of his own. This happens. Saul was not changed at once. He became worse first. But he had *watched* Stephen die. God's pursuit of Saul had begun.

vv. 5 through 13

*Then Philip went down to the city of Samaria, and preached Christ unto them. And the people with one accord gave heed unto those things which Philip spake, hearing and seeing the miracles which he did. . . . But there was a certain man, called Simon, which beforetime in the same city used sorcery, and bewitched the people of Samaria, giving out that himself was some great one:*

*To whom they all gave heed, from the least to the greatest, saying, This man is the great power of God. . . . But when they believed Philip preaching the things concerning the kingdom of God, and the name of Jesus Christ, they were baptized, both men and women. Then Simon himself believed also: and when he was baptized, he continued with Philip, and wondered, beholding the miracles and signs which were done.*

It is interesting and hopeful that Simon "believed . . . was baptized [and] continued with Philip." All of these are good signs. At the same time he "wondered, beholding the miracles and signs which were done." Now, there is surely nothing wrong with Simon's being impressed with the miracles Philip performed. After all, this had been Simon's profession too. There is nothing unusual in the fact that the miracle-working would have intrigued him more than any other aspect of his new faith. It would intrigue anyone so new in the kingdom. It is no indication to me of any lack of sincerity on Simon's part—merely an indication of his conditioning. But the remainder of the story about Simon indicates that he was still in some darkness.

vv. 14 through 19

*Now when the apostles which were at Jerusalem heard that Samaria had received the word of God, they sent unto them Peter and John: Who, when they were come down, prayed for them, that they might receive the Holy Ghost: (For as yet he was fallen upon none of them: only they were baptized in the name of the Lord Jesus.) Then laid they their hands on them, and they received the Holy Ghost. And when Simon saw that through laying on of the apostles' hands the Holy Ghost was given, he offered them money, Saying, Give me also this power, that on whomsoever I lay hands, he may receive the Holy Ghost.*

There is no doubt here that Simon, although he had "believed" and was baptized by Philip, was still in hot pursuit of glory for himself—power for his own use. He had barely set his foot on the Way. As many today, after years of "believing" and years after baptism, have merely set their feet on the Way. Simon, as I see him, had made an intellectual decision to follow Christ, but was still just standing there. He had not begun to walk.

vv. 20 through 23

*But Peter said unto him, Thy money perish with thee, because thou hast thought that the gift of God may be purchased with money. Thou hast neither part nor lot in this matter: for thy heart is not right in the sight of God. Repent therefore of this thy wickedness, and pray God, if perhaps the thought of thine heart may be forgiven thee. For I perceive that thou art in the gall of bitterness, and in the bond of iniquity.*

Let us glance away from Simon for a moment in order to take a quick look at how Peter handled this new believer. What he said to Simon is true. The man had missed the point entirely. But to me it is interesting to note that even though he had been filled with the Spirit, Peter could still revert to his old impetuous manner. He spoke the truth, but this time he did not speak it in anything resembling tenderness or gentleness. There is always the possibility, of course, that Peter had learned that Simon, the sorcerer, only responded to plain talk—brusqueness. Yet it is fascinating to me that God does not always completely alter human personality. I think he seldom alters it entirely. He is not about the business of making us carbon copies of what we think of as "saints." God is about the eternal business of living his life in us through his Holy Spirit so that we can begin to be the very best we can be within our human limitations.

v. 24

*Then answered Simon, and said, Pray ye to the Lord for me, that none of these things which ye have spoken come upon me.*

Simon is still thinking of Simon, but at least he had the grace and humility to ask for prayer. We are not told what eventually happened to Simon's faith, but because I can so easily identify with his mixed motives, I have to be hopeful about him.

v. 25

*And they, when they had testified and preached the word of the Lord, returned to Jersualem, and preached the gospel in many villages of the Samaritans.*

It is well to remember, in view of our race-relations problems of today, that the Samaritans hated the Jews. The members of the early Church must have shown

love, or they would not have been received. Their
Master had preceded them into Samaria, and John and
Peter and the other Twelve were with him there. The
Samaritans must have seen Christ's love in them by his
Spirit which had invaded their lives.

v. 26

*And the angel of the Lord spake unto Philip, saying,
Arise, and go toward the south unto the way that goeth
down from Jerusalem unto Gaza, which is desert.*

Does God speak to us directly? So directly that we
would change our route and go by another road—a
road seldom used by other travelers? Is it really possible
that a mere human being filled with the Spirit of God
can be guided in this specific way? Frequently I receive
—out of the blue—entire manuscripts from would-be
writers who insist that God has "told" them to write.
Of course, editing is not my profession, but when there
is time to scan a page or two, this is enough to let me
know that God simply could not have "told" the person
to write because ninety-nine times out of a hundred
he or she is no writer. God has no need for any more
inferior efforts. Often the subject matter, while it may
be sprinkled with religious terminology, is off-center,
marginal, fanatic in its emphasis. Or it is so totally self-
centered as to be neurotic. I also receive letters from
persons who need a speaker for some particularly important meeting—one they obviously look forward to
with great eagerness. They have been assigned the job

of getting a speaker, and "The Lord has told us specifically that you are the one. I feel sure, Miss Price, that if you pray about it, you will come to us." In other words, if I am writing and can't come or if I am already committed elsewhere on that date, I *must* be disobeying God. This is a ticklish thing. We need to be very realistic and honest when we attempt to get our guidance from on high. Actually, after more than twenty years as a follower of Jesus Christ, who indwells me by his Spirit too, I have become convinced that if a human heart is surrendered to his heart, God doesn't mind whether that disciple goes about being God's friend in Africa or Germany or New York. It seems more logical and more like Jesus Christ to conclude that *wherever we are,* he wants to teach us particularized love for those whom our lives touch.

None of this means that I believe he never gives us detailed directions. He does. There are certain circumstances where he must. But we weaken our own spirits when we fool around waiting for handwriting on the wall. God makes marvelously creative use even of our mistakes. His main interest is the condition of our hearts—not the route number of the road on which we drive our cars.

Still, I believe the circumstance of Philip's encounter with the Ethiopian authority was such that God did speak plainly to him. A few times in my years with Christ, he has guided me specifically. Mainly, he guides by the measure of our friendship with him.

Our part is to stay in open fellowship with the

Source of all wisdom—learning, learning daily how to be natural with God, learning how to be his friend. We are never on a hot seat with a real friend, chewing our nails wondering what will please him and what will displease him. We are comfortable with our real friends because we know them. If you are agitating because you haven't received your "guidance" for something, put it aside for the time being and concentrate on learning more of what Jesus Christ is really like. As with Philip, there is at certain times definite direction, but I believe that God has a right to expect us to learn to use our Spirit-enlightened intelligence.

vv. 27 through 31

*And he [Philip] arose and went: and, behold, a man of Ethiopia, an eunuch of great authority under Candace queen of the Ethiopians, who had the charge of all her treasure, and had come to Jerusalem for to worship, Was returning, and sitting in his chariot read Esaias the prophet. Then the Spirit said unto Philip, Go near, and join thyself to this chariot. And Philip ran thither to him, and heard him read the prophet Esaias, and said, Understandest thou what thou readest? And he said, How can I, except some man should guide me? And he desired Philip that he would come up and sit with him.*

Now undoubtedly the Spirit of God guided Philip specifically that day. Being God, he knew that the Ethiopian was on that particular road. Being God, he also knew that the man's heart was open and receptive.

(There would be no need for Philip to behave like a heavy-handed "personal worker!") God also knew about the wide sphere of influence this man held in his own country. He needed the Ethiopian. The Ethiopian needed God. He guided Philip to him.

> vv. 32 through 35
>
> *The place of the scripture which he read was this, He was led as a sheep to the slaughter; and like a lamb dumb before his shearer, so opened he not his mouth: In his humiliation his judgment was taken away: and who shall declare his generation? for his life is taken from the earth. And the eunuch answered Philip, and said, I pray thee, of whom speaketh the prophet this? of himself, or of some other man? Then Philip opened his mouth, and began at the same scripture, and preached unto him Jesus.*

This encounter must have been one of the happiest and most exciting of Philip's life. He was one of the seven chosen with Stephen to be a servant to the widows and the poor. For his willingness to serve, to handle food supplies and other necessary provisions, to help keep the peace among the faithful by seeing to it that the Grecian widows were treated as well as the Hebrew widows—for being willing to be all things to all men, even to preaching and traveling and healing when the occasion arose—God gave Philip this beautiful encounter with the Ethiopian. I can't think of any kind of experience that would bring more joy to a disciple than this: A learned man, with influence among his own people, a hungry heart and his scroll open to the fifty-third chapter of Isaiah! The eunuch's question went straight to the heart of the Christian faith: "Who is this? Tell me the name of this man who was led as a sheep to the slaughter? What is his name?"

"Then Philip . . . preached unto him Jesus." Quite probably this man took true Christianity to his native Africa because Philip met him that day. But to me, the beauty of the incident lies in the amazing, God-ordered symmetry of the encounter: an intelligent, in-quiring mind, open to truth, reading truth without knowing it, but wanting to know; matched with this, a God-guided messenger with an open, uncondemning heart, time to talk and the truth to unfold. The influen-tial Ethiopian and Philip and God. The meeting of these three on that little-traveled desert road rivals any art piece, any music, any literature in the pure form and symmetry of the Spirit. There was nothing off-key, nothing out of balance. It was all there.

vv. 36 and 37

*And as they went on their way, they came unto a certain water: and the eunuch said, See, here is water; what doth hinder me to be baptized? And Philip said, If thou believest with all thine heart, thou mayest. And he answered and said, I believe that Jesus Christ is the Son of God.*

It was all there, the central truth: Jesus is God, the articulated faith, the act.

vv. 38 and 39

*And he commanded the chariot to stand still: and they went down both into the water, both Philip and the eunuch; and he baptized him. And when they were come up out of the water, the Spirit of the Lord caught away Philip, that the eunuch saw him no more: and he went on his way rejoicing.*

It was all there—and the rejoicing.

 CHAPTER 9

vv. 1 and 2

*And Saul, yet breathing out threatenings and slaughter against the disciples of the Lord, went unto the high priest, And desired of him letters to Damascus to the synagogues, that if he found any of this way, whether they were men or women, he might bring them bound unto Jerusalem.*

As the rulers of the temple who stood at Jesus' cross watching him die grew more and more enraged, so did Saul, who had watched Jesus' disciple, Stephen, die. The King James Version cannot be improved upon here: "Saul, yet breathing out threatenings and slaughter. . . ." To destroy the believers in Christ had become his very breath.

vv. 3 through 5

*And as he [Saul] journeyed, he came near Damascus: and suddenly there shined round about him a light from heaven: And he fell to the earth, and heard a*

*voice saying unto him, Saul, Saul, why persecutest thou*
*me? And he said, Who art thou, Lord? And the Lord*
*said, I am Jesus whom thou persecutest: it is hard for*
*thee to kick against the pricks.*

The impact of that sudden Presence of love against
the hate in Saul was enough to knock a man to the
ground. Saul was a religionist. He believed himself to
be serving the Lord God of Israel when he persecuted
the disciples of Jesus. His service had become an obses-
sion. Now, in that terrible moment of light, the proud
spirit cracked. The brilliant, highly educated student
of Gamaliel did not take time for reason or for logic.
On his knees in the dusty road, he heard himself call
this Jesus "Lord": "Who art thou, Lord?"

Most of the modern translations omit the line the
King James Version indicates Jesus spoke: "it is hard
for thee to kick against the pricks." This line, whether
it was in the original writings or not, has meaning for
me. It is like Jesus. He is, even at this stunning moment
of encounter with the hate-filled Saul, showing Saul
that he understands how destructive this pursuit of
violence has been for a sensitive man to follow. Without knowing it, Saul had been persecuting the God he
meant to be serving. It was tearing him apart inwardly,
destroying him. The Lord knew this, and he let Saul
know that he knew.

vv. 6 through 9

*And he trembling and astonished said, Lord, what*
*wilt thou have me to do? And the Lord said unto him,*

*Arise, and go into the city, and it shall be told thee what thou must do. And the men which journeyed with him stood speechless, hearing a voice, but seeing no man. And Saul arose from the earth; and when his eyes were opened, he saw no man: but they led him by the hand, and brought him into Damascus. And he was three days without sight, and neither did eat nor drink.*

Saul not only instantly called Jesus "Lord"; he immediately obeyed Jesus' command to "go into the city" —obeyed and, obviously as suddenly, *believed*. The shock of discovering who it was he had been persecuting blinded the young man, but he permitted himself to be led by the hand in total obedience with what Jesus had said to him.

It has always been a fascination to me to try to imagine what Paul *thought* during the three days he was "without sight" or food or drink. Having experienced a definite moment of conversion myself (and not all do, of course) , I can comprehend something of the wonder, the mystery, the altogether new sense of worship which must have filled his mind. In a definite sense, Saul *lived* on the new awareness of God's identity. There were surely moments of deep remorse and repentance, but I doubt that he suffered only the pain of actual guilt during those first three days. I believe the wonder was too great.

vv. 10 through 12

*And there was a certain disciple at Damascus, named Ananias; and to him said the Lord in a vision, Ananias.*

*And he said, Behold, I am here, Lord. And the Lord said unto him, Arise, and go into the street which is called Straight, and enquire in the house of Judas for one called Saul, of Tarsus: for, behold, he prayeth, And hath seen in a vision a man named Ananias coming in, and putting his hand on him, that he might receive his sight.*

The interesting line here is "for, behold, he prayeth." Jesus knew that Ananias, no matter how deep his loyalty, would be afraid of Saul, the persecutor of Christians. And it would seem that the fear should drop away if Ananias saw Saul praying. This was not true then, and it is not true now. Prayer still serves too many purposes for man. Saul was known to be religious. To see him at prayer would not quiet Ananias' anxiety.

vv. 15 and 16

*But the Lord said unto him, Go thy way: for he is a chosen vessel unto me, to bear my name before the Gentiles, and kings, and the children of Israel: For I will shew him how great things he must suffer for my name's sake.*

Ananias (in verses 13 and 14) explained his fears to the Lord, and then Jesus did what he so often does: He gave the anxious disciple a specific explanation: "for he [Saul] is a chosen vessel unto me, to bear my name. . . ." Up to that point, Ananias had been thinking (quite naturally) in terms of his own service and safety. But the Lord got down to particulars, reminding him that He needed this man, Saul, for His own purposes. This shifted Ananias' attention from himself to God and (verse 17) he went on his way, and laid his hands on Saul, praying for him to receive his sight and to be filled with the Holy Spirit.

vv. 18 and 19

*And immediately there fell from his eyes as it had been scales: and he received sight forthwith, and arose, and was baptized. And when he had received meat, he was strengthened. Then was Saul certain days with the disciples which were at Damascus.*

It is interesting to me that, when no disciple was available, Jesus appeared personally to Saul and to Ananias. But when possible, God uses a human intermediary. It is also interesting and (with simple believers, *natural*) to do what Saul did once he could see again and once he was filled with the Spirit: He looked up other Christians, the very men he was on his way to Damascus to persecute!

v. 20

*And straightway he preached Christ in the synagogues, that he is the Son of God.*

This to me is the most dynamic verse in the entire story of Saul's conversion. He started out on center with Christ only, and throughout his entire life the great Apostle stayed on center. He began "straightway" to preach that Jesus Christ is the Son of God, and nothing moved Saul (Paul) from this one Absolute. He treated the marginal issues in his teaching programs with the young churches, but inevitably he returned to the only essential: Jesus Christ himself.

vv. 23 through 25

*And after that many days were fulfilled, the Jews took counsel to kill him: But their laying await was known of Saul. And they watched the gates day and night to kill him. Then the disciples took him by night, and let him down by the wall in a basket.*

Of course, the non-Christian Jews wanted Saul out of the way. He was more than just another disciple causing trouble by his preaching that Jesus was the Son of God; he was, to them, an out-and-out traitor.

Here again, God never uses visions and miracles if he can make use of the ordinary: Saul escaped death by way of a basket on the end of a rope.

v. 26

*And when Saul was come to Jerusalem, he assayed to join himself to the disciples: but they were all afraid of him, and believed not that he was a disciple.*

Saul even had to prove himself to those who already followed Christ. This, however, is not so unusual as it may appear at first glance. Even relatively new believers, mainly because of what to long-time Christians is "strange" conditioning, still must do this now and then. After twenty years of following Christ publicly, I still have to answer letters from those who are suddenly "suspicious" of me. "I no longer consider you a disciple of Jesus Christ after reading your novel, *New Moon Rising*," a lady wrote. The book ends with what to me is a conversion, but it sounded strange to her. Christians today are no different from the Christians Saul knew.

vv. 27 through 31

*But Barnabas took him, and brought him to the apostles, and declared unto them how he had seen the Lord in the way, and that he had spoken to him, and how he had preached boldly at Damascus in the name of Jesus. And he was with them coming in and going out at Jerusalem. And he spake boldly in the name of the Lord Jesus. . . . Then had the churches rest throughout all Judaea and Galilee and Samaria, and were edified; and walking in the fear of the Lord, and in the comfort of the Holy Ghost, were multiplied.*

One of their own, Barnabas, had to come to Saul's rescue. Apparently, even with the Twelve, Saul had to be vouched for. As with some of us, they seemed to have a hard time believing that Jesus Christ can change a man as much as he had obviously changed Saul.

vv. 36 through 40 (Read through v. 43.)

*Now there was at Joppa a certain disciple named Tabitha, which by interpretation is called Dorcas: this woman was full of good works and almsdeeds which she did. And it came to pass in those days, that she was sick, and died: . . . And forasmuch as Lydda was nigh to Joppa, and the disciples had heard that Peter was there, they sent unto him two men, desiring him that he would not delay to come to them. Then Peter arose and went with them. When he was come, they brought him into the upper chamber: and all the widows stood by him weeping, and shewing the coats and garments which Dorcas made, while she was with them. But Peter put them all forth, and kneeled down, and prayed; and turning him to the body said, Tabitha, arise. And she opened her eyes: and when she saw Peter, she sat up.*

I do not believe that the Lord raised Dorcas from the dead through Peter merely because she had worked hard to make a lot of coats and garments for the poor. Millions of women in the history of Christianity have been as faithful and unselfish as Dorcas and were not raised from the dead. We err when we attempt to pin God down in this superficial manner by some pat explanation man can accept. I have no theory as to why they did not have to bury Dorcas that day, other than the fact that so often, when one of the disciples permitted God to perform a miracle through him, numbers began to believe. There was no better way to convince the skeptic then. God is not unmindful of what methods are effective at a given time in the stubborn history of his loved ones.

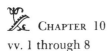 CHAPTER 10

vv. 1 through 8

*There was a certain man in Caesarea called Cornelius . . . A devout man, and one that feared God with all his house, which gave much alms to the people, and prayed to God alway. He saw in a vision evidently about the ninth hour of the day an angel of God coming in to him, and saying unto him, Cornelius. And when he looked on him, he was afraid, and said, What is it, Lord? And he said unto him, Thy prayers and thine alms are come up for a memorial before God. . . . send men to Joppa, and call for one Simon, whose surname is Peter: He lodgeth with one Simon a tanner, whose house is by the sea side: he shall tell thee what thou oughtest to do. And when the angel . . . was departed, he called two of his household servants, and a devout soldier of them that waited on him continually; And when he had declared all these things unto them, he sent them to Joppa.*

Contrary to the point of view of many rigid Christians, God can and does "get through" to men and women whose hearts are open to him, but who may not have total New Testament light on their paths. Cornelius truly worshiped all he knew of the Lord God. As far as he saw, he acted.

Here again, because there were no enlightened disciples around, God had to resort to supernatural means of communicating with Cornelius. But He was sending him to talk to Peter.

v. 9

*On the morrow, as they went on their journey, and drew nigh unto the city, Peter went up upon the house-top to pray about the sixth hour:*

As he is now, God was then acting, directing, prompting men within their familiar framework of *time*. He lives in the *eternal now*, but he never forgets that we are time-bound.

vv. 10 through 16

*And he [Peter] became very hungry, and would have eaten: but while they made ready, he fell into a trance, And saw heaven opened, and a certain vessel descending unto him, as it had been a great sheet knit at the four corners, and let down to the earth: Wherein were all manner of fourfooted beasts of the earth, and wild beasts, and creeping things, and fowls of the air. And there came a voice to him, Rise, Peter; kill, and eat. But Peter said, Not so, Lord; for I have never eaten any thing that is common or unclean. And the voice spake unto him again the second time, What God hath cleansed, that call not thou common. This was done thrice: and the vessel was received up again into heaven.*

The first thing that strikes me here is that God knew Peter through and through. He chose a time when Peter was his most vulnerable—early in the morning, before breakfast (while breakfast was being prepared), to begin teaching him the central Christian lesson of brotherhood. So conditioned by his early training, which centered around the superiority of the Jews as God's chosen people, Peter needed some means which would strike him "where he lived" to crack this patronizing shell of hereditary righteousness. God picked out a time when Peter's mind was on food and let down the big sheet full of things to eat. Of course, when Peter refused, he felt utterly "spiritual." Until this moment, he had been convinced that God agreed with his ancestors concerning their superiority to Gentiles and all other races. Being God, He patiently repeated the command three times. And then the vision vanished, and Peter had a few minutes to think it through.

vv. 17 through 20

*Now while Peter doubted in himself what this vision . . . should mean, behold, the men which were sent from Cornelius had made enquiry for Simon's house, and stood before the gate, And called, and asked whether Simon, which was surnamed Peter, were lodged there. While Peter thought on the vision, the Spirit said unto him, Behold, three men seek thee. Arise therefore, and get thee down, and go with them, doubting nothing: for I have sent them.*

God knew exactly where the messengers from Cornelius were on the way, and he knew exactly where Peter was—in his confusion. He gave Peter what he still gives us: the chance to learn a truth by acting on it in blind faith in the nature of God. I am learning, as the years go by, to go ahead whether I understand God's reasoning or not. Authentic faith is based not on our understanding of God's directions, but on our understanding of what he is really like. This, of course, is the reason no one lives adequately unless he or she is concentrating on the continuous discovery of the nature of God in Jesus Christ. There is no other specific way to learn God's nature. This is why Jesus came to earth.

v. 21

> *Then Peter went down to the men which were sent unto him from Cornelius; and said, Behold, I am he whom ye seek: what is the cause wherefore ye are come?*

Peter was acting on what he knew of the very nature of the God who had been trying to teach him such a surprising facet of truth. I like Peter because obviously he was no spiritual giant. He was just plain "people" like us. But he had lived with Jesus of Nazareth during his time on earth, had been the first to catch on to the central truth that "thou art that Christ, the Son of the living God"—and so, because of what Peter knew of the nature of this God, he obeyed His command, though still doubting, still mostly in the dark as to what God was up to. In verses 22 and 23, the men explained about Cornelius and their mission, Peter took them in for the night, called for a few of the brothers who lived in Joppa to go with him on the strange journey, and set out for Caesarea.

vv. 24 through 26

> *And the morrow after they entered into Caesarea. And Cornelius waited for them, and had called together his kinsmen and near friends. And as Peter was coming in, Cornelius met him, and fell down at his feet, and worshipped him. But Peter took him up, saying, Stand up; I myself also am a man.*

Peter had this much straight. A tiny crack in his ancient concept of the superiority of his own race had been made the day he was shown on the road to Philippi with Jesus that his Master *was* God in the flesh. This freed Peter of at least some of his exclusiveness. We are all born to worship, not to be worshiped. He had found a Master who satisfied his normal human desire to adore another. He discovered, as anyone can in that moment of realization about Jesus, that we are merely human, as is any other mortal. Nothing could have been more out of line to Peter than to have a man worship him. Peter was a believer in the Godship of Jesus Christ. He would never again be able to worship a great man, even a human king. The first crack in Peter's hereditary armor had been made: "Stand up, man! I am only a man too."

vv. 27 through 29

*And as he talked with him, he went in, and found many that were come together. And he said unto them, Ye know how that it is an unlawful thing for a man that is a Jew to keep company, or come unto one of another nation; but God hath shewed me that I should not call any man common or unclean. Therefore came I unto you without gainsaying, as soon as I was sent for: I ask therefore for what intent ye have sent for me?*

Peter grew a hundred cubits in that moment. Even if perhaps he was secretly hoping that Cornelius and his friends might think him a bighearted fellow for being so humble as to walk right into their Gentile house, still Peter spoke what for him was an entirely new, earthshaking truth. And he spoke it *after* he had acted upon it. "Therefore came I unto you." He didn't go about "preaching brotherhood" and spouting off about his special vision from God. He acted first and then articulated what God had just taught him. At that moment, Peter was indeed being God's friend—far more than a servant, a friend. Addressing men and women who had up to *yesterday* been unclean and common to him, Peter actually stood inside their house asking, "What may I do for you?"

In the remaining verses of Chapter 10, truth, the whole truth about God's visit to the earth in Jesus, broke over the roomful of people because another facet of that Truth had broken over Peter that day. Historically, it was an important moment in the life of the Church, but to me the dynamic of the story is that God chose the most headstrong Apostle, Peter, to begin to move love abroad in the world. Peter could well have been like some headstrong segregationists today—not a cruel man, but so certain of his own racial superiority that God knew to convince Peter would be ultimately to convince a world.

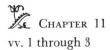 CHAPTER 11

vv. 1 through 3

*And the apostles and brethren that were in Judaea heard that the Gentiles had also received the word of God. And when Peter was come up to Jerusalem, they*

*that were of the circumcision contended with him, Say-*
*ing, Thou wentest in to men uncircumcised, and didst*
*eat with them.*

This is so familiar to this day as to call forth a loud
"Ho hum." The "apostles and brethren" didn't want
any new "brothers" who deviated one iota from what
they believed. No one could congratulate Peter on his
new insight because all of them were in too much darkness themselves to recognize it as such. Rather, they
jumped on him for eating with "unclean" people.

"I can't possibly have fellowship with *him*—he
drinks or smokes or was baptized the wrong way! No
man is *my* brother until he holds exactly the same doctrine about the Lord Jesus Christ that I hold!" Sound
familiar? A complaint still repeating itself down
through the years from the day Peter was attacked by
those who professed to believe in the heart that broke
on Calvary, who professed to believe in the stretched-
out arms—stretched out on a cross to encompass and
welcome the world which "God so loved."

I can only thank this One of the stretched-out arms
and the torn-open heart that the complainer's half-truth
about him is just that—half truth, minus his mercy and
his patience and his understanding.

vv. 4, 17 and 18

*But Peter rehearsed the matter from the beginning,*
*and expounded it by order unto them, saying [in sum-*
*mary]. . . . Forasmuch then as God gave them the like*
*gift as he did unto us, who believed on the Lord*

*Jesus Christ; what was I, that I could withstand God? When they heard these things, they held their peace, and glorified God, saying, Then hath God also to the Gentiles granted repentance unto life.*

Hurray for those "apostles and brethren"! And hurray, I say, for Peter. He must have lived well before them because once he told them, step by step, exactly what had happened on the rooftop in his vision and at Cornelius' house, they believed him. Peter told them that he saw these Gentiles filled with the same familiar Spirit. Peter's word held. He did not compromise in the telling. He made no effort to be falsely "humble." He didn't say, "Now, I'm not altogether sure about these people—we'll have to watch them for a while and see." He put no one on trial. He had no reservations. He had seen with his own eyes and he told them what he knew to be true. Shocking as it must have been to them all—as it was to Peter—the big fisherman had seen God in Gentiles. "Who was I, then, to try to stop God?" (*Good News for Modern Man*)

vv. 22, 24 and 25

*Then tidings of these things came unto the ears of the church which was in Jerusalem: and they sent forth Barnabas, that he should go as far as Antioch. . . . For he was a good man, and full of the Holy Ghost and of faith: and much people was added unto the Lord. Then departed Barnabas to Tarsus, for to seek Saul: And when he had found him, he brought him unto Antioch. And it came to pass, that a whole year they assembled themselves with the church, and taught much people. And the disciples were called Christians first in Antioch.*

Once Peter saw that God loved Gentiles too, the early Church began to spread like wildfire, not only because including Gentiles increased the "harvest field," but because the full operative power of love had been set free in the world.

I am fascinated by the special mention of the kind of man Barnabas was: "a good man, and full of the Holy Ghost and of faith." The Holy Ghost is God's life in us, and surely Barnabas was filled with the very perception of God. Remember (Chapter 9, verse 27) that it was Barnabas who, seeing in Saul of Tarsus a man filled with God—even a few days after his conversion—took him to the skeptical Apostles and convinced them that he was a true believer. Saul must have made a deep impression on Barnabas then. It is obvious that a deep friendship sprang up between the two men, because now that the need for active disciples was so great, Barnabas went to Tarsus to get Saul to help him in Antioch.

And, I think, most appropriately—because of the new believer, Saul, and the "good man," Barnabas—it was at Antioch that followers of the Way began to be called Christians.

vv. 27 through 30

*And in these days came prophets from Jerusalem unto Antioch. And there stood up one of them named*

*Agabus, and signified by the Spirit that there should be great dearth throughout all the world: which came to pass in the days of Claudius Caesar. Then the disciples, every man according to his ability, determined to send relief unto the brethren which dwelt in Judaea: Which also they did, and sent it to the elders by the hands of Barnabas and Saul.*

It is appropriate also that these two friends (Saul and Barnabas) were the first Christian caseworkers.

 Chapter 12

vv. 1 and 2

*Now about that time Herod the king stretched forth his hands to vex certain of the church. And he killed James the brother of John with the sword.*

Until now, I hadn't thought about John, the beloved disciple, in connection with the murder of his brother, James. Both men were Jesus' first cousins—their mothers were sisters. And all through their ministry with Jesus before his death, these brothers were always mentioned together in one breath. Jesus thought of them that way, even to the amusing nickname he gave them: sons of thunder. John's grief must have been inexplicable, and undoubtedly, as grief can do for those who know Christ, it helped prepare him to write his simple, loving Gospel and the short letters so filled with the love of God himself.

vv. 3 through 8

*And because he [Herod] saw it pleased the Jews, he proceeded further to take Peter also . . . he put him in prison, and delivered him to four quaternions of soldiers [sixteen] to keep him; intending after Easter to bring him forth to the people. Peter therefore was kept in prison: but prayer was made without ceasing of the church unto God for him. And when Herod would have brought him forth, the same night Peter was sleeping between two soldiers, bound with two chains: and the keepers before the door kept the prison. And, behold, the angel of the Lord came upon him, and a light shined in the prison: and he smote Peter on the side, and raised him up, saying, Arise up quickly. And his chains fell off from his hands. And the angel said unto him, Gird thyself, and bind on thy sandals. And so he did. And he saith unto him, Cast thy garment about thee, and follow me.*

The wonder here to me has always been not that God managed Peter's escape from prison—God can do anything—but that he once more proved himself to be minutely loving, caring for the smallest detail of Peter's welfare. "Gird thyself, and bind on thy sandals. . . . Cast thy garment about thee. . . ." Get dressed, Peter, my son. Put on your shoes and don't forget your coat. God's tenderness is far more transforming than what we think of as power.

vv. 9 through 11

*And he went out, and followed him; and wist not that it was true which was done by the angel; but thought he saw a vision. When they were past the first and the second ward, they came unto the iron gate that leadeth unto the city; which opened to them of his own accord: and they went out, and passed on through one street; and forthwith the angel departed from him. And when Peter was come to himself, he said, Now I know of a surety, that the Lord hath sent his angel, and hath delivered me out of the hand of Herod. . . .*

Understanding Peter, God's angel walked with him not only all the way out of the prison, but up one familiar street, making sure that Peter knew it was not a dream. Again, we can find easy affinity with Peter who, in spite of all he had seen the Lord do before, still thought he must be dreaming this time.

v. 12

*And when he had considered the thing, he came to the house of Mary the mother of John, whose surname was Mark: where many were gathered together praying.*

As soon as Peter realized the predicament he was in, he knew he needed to find a safe place. God used an angel to do what the praying disciples at Mark's mother's house could not do—open the doors of the prison. But now Peter knew God well enough to begin to act on his own human intelligence. He was not safe from the authorities just because God had let him out into the streets.

vv. 13 and 14

*And as Peter knocked at the door of the gate, a damsel came to hearken, named Rhoda. And when she*

*knew Peter's voice, she opened not the gate for glad-*
*ness, but ran in, and told how Peter stood before the*
*gate.*

In *The Unique World of Women* I have written at
length about Rhoda, the slave girl of Mary, Mark's
mother, and I concluded that Rhoda was not stupid—
just young and somewhat scatterbrained—and so ex-
cited to recognize Peter's voice that she simply didn't
use her head enough to let him come inside to safety.
She had to tell her news first. I think this is really all
that's here, except that it is obvious that Rhoda had a
real capacity for joy and excitement—a capacity we all
need.

vv. 15 and 16

*And they said unto her [Rhoda], Thou art mad.*
*But she constantly affirmed that it was even so. Then*
*said they, It is his angel. But Peter continued knock-*
*ing: and when they had opened the door, and saw*
*him, they were astonished.*

Silly girl! She's crazy! Even God could not manage to
have Peter out of prison and knocking on their door.
It *has* to be his angel standing there. It can't be Peter!

v. 17

*But he [Peter], beckoning unto them with the hand*
*to hold their peace, declared unto them how the*
*Lord had brought him out of the prison. And he said,*
*Go shew these things unto James, and to the brethren.*
*And he departed, and went into another place.*

Peter had not run to Mary's house only for safety, but to let the disciples know their prayers had been answered—and to send word to James, the brother of Jesus, who now headed the church in Jerusalem. James had not believed that his elder brother, Jesus, had come from God during Jesus' earthly lifetime, but when the Lord made a point of appearing to James (I Corinthians 15:7) after His Resurrection, James believed and now had become a leader in his brother's church. Peter wanted it known that God had once more protected his own. Only after that did he go "into another place" to preach where it would be safer—at least until the present trouble blew over.

v. 25

*And Barnabas and Saul returned from Jerusalem, when they had fulfilled their ministry, and took with them John, whose surname was Mark.*

Here, in the action-packed story of the new Church, is where Saul—soon to be renamed Paul—came into his own. He was already a leader in need of an assistant. He chose Barnabas' nephew, John Mark.

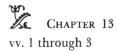 CHAPTER 13

vv. 1 through 3

*Now there were in the church that was at Antioch certain prophets and teachers; as Barnabas, and Simeon that was called Niger, and Lucius of Cyrene, and*

*Manaen . . . and Saul. As they ministered to the Lord, and fasted, the Holy Ghost said, Separate me Barnabas and Saul for the work whereunto I have called them. And when they had fasted and prayed, and laid their hands on them, they sent them away.*

The bond was already there, humanly speaking, between Barnabas and Saul. It is the same whether God caused their friendship to spring up knowing he would send them out together, or whether he sent them to work as a team because he knew of their close relationship.

vv. 4 and 5

*So they, being sent forth by the Holy Ghost, departed unto Seleucia; and from thence they sailed to Cyprus. And when they were at Salamis, they preached the word of God in the synagogues of the Jews: and they had also John to their minister.*

This rather awkward wording in the King James, "and they had also John to their minister," simply means that Mary's young son, John Mark, went along to minister to Barnabas and Saul and to help in the work in any way he might be needed. John Mark was quite young, perhaps still a teen-ager. His mother, Mary of Jerusalem, must have been happy to see her son under the influence of two men like Paul and Barnabas.

vv. 6 through 12

*And when they had gone through the isle unto Paphos, they found a certain sorcerer, a false prophet, a Jew, whose name was Bar-jesus: Which was with the deputy [Governor] of the country, Sergius Paulus, a prudent man; who called for Barnabas and Saul, and desired to hear the word of God. But Elymas the sorcerer [his name in Greek] withstood them, seeking to turn away the deputy from the faith. Then Saul, (who also is called Paul,) filled with the Holy Ghost, set his eyes on him, And said, O full of all subtilty and all mischief, thou child of the devil, thou enemy of all righteousness, wilt thou not cease to pervert the right ways of the Lord? And now, behold, the hand of the Lord is upon thee, and thou shalt be blind, not seeing the sun for a season. And immediately there fell on him a mist and a darkness; and he went about seeking some to lead him by the hand.*

This passage is one of the many in the Bible (more in the Old Testament, of course, than in the New) where I cannot reconcile what I read with what I have learned about the nature of God in Jesus Christ from the same New Testament. The Scriptures say that Paul was filled with the Holy Ghost when he lashed out at the sorcerer. Well, as I see it, the Holy Ghost is not likely to do anything that Jesus wouldn't do. Jesus did say (John 16:8a) that when the Holy Ghost came, he would "reprove the world of sin. . . ." Paul was not acting in a contradictory way when he informed Elymas of his sinful behavior. But would Jesus have struck a man blind? Did he blind Saul? Didn't he go about bringing sight to blind eyes? Some will say, "But God must have done it through Paul—a mere man cannot cause another man to go suddenly blind." I don't know.

Sorcerers, those who dabble in the occult either as a hobby or professionally, are much in the news these days. People are buying their books in far greater quantities than they buy books about Jesus Christ. And surely some of those who operate in the world of the occult are—or at least seem to be—evil people. Some, of course, are not. I feel that the occult is often a substitute for faith and, for that reason, it is dangerous. Yet one of America's most famous soothsayers, Jeanne Dixon, is a Christian. There is no point in arguing the wrong or the right of the use of the occult here. My thoughts are quite open-end on it, anyway at this point. And this is one of the new freedoms I am finding in God. I no longer need to have it all decided. I no longer need to fear the criticism of God's people if I don't happen to be as certain of someone's sinful pursuits as they are. I need only fear God, and he is going right along with me on my pilgrimage toward deeper understanding, approving the fact, I believe, that I am never again going to be satisfied with pat answers.

So I do not disagree with Paul for telling the man off. I have to admit that I am puzzled by the "punishment," though it is possible that the man suffered sudden (and commonplace) hysterical blindness—as perhaps occurred to Saul on the Damascus road. I can only say that this strange happening strikes me as more like Paul's opinion of what the man deserved than God's. After all, Paul was an intense, once utterly self-righteous, man. I've never known a conversion to change anyone entirely, just like that. If Paul lost all his overriding, opinionated, violent characteristics overnight, I think he must have been the first one. The great Apostle (to me the greatest) is a favorite of mine for this reason: He remained the honed intellectual, and it would have been a miracle indeed if he had become a patient saint in a flash.

v. 12

*Then the deputy [Governor], when he saw what was done, believed, being astonished at the doctrine of the Lord.*

At any rate, Paul got his man, the Governor. I'm frankly confused at the fact that seeing a man go blind should clear up the "doctrine of the Lord," but any passage such as this which forces us to get down to the nitty-gritty where God's character is concerned is cause for joy—as is any passage that *dares* us to think.

v. 13

*Now when Paul and his company loosed from Paphos, they came to Perga in Pamphylia: and John [Mark] departing from them returned to Jerusalem.*

I am terribly curious as to what really happened between Paul and John Mark, but of two things we can be sure: John Mark was young and impulsive, and Paul *was* a new Christian still. It is not at all farfetched to observe that Paul must have been like most of the rest of us when that first Light breaks suddenly: almost obnoxious in our certainty, our desire to convince— fast. I do not worship Paul. Some almost seem to, simply because he wrote so many of the Scriptures. This would have broken his heart—he whose very life was not his own spiritual experience, but Jesus Christ. "To me to live is Christ." A man who could write that would loathe being worshiped as a perfect human being. He never forgot that he felt he was "the chiefest of sinners." Of course, he wasn't. No one is. Or is everyone? But, as I see it, this is Paul admitting that he got in his own way often, and this could have had a lot to do with John Mark's going home to Jerusalem.

v. 49 (Read Paul's sermons at Antioch, vv. 14 through 47.)

*And the word of the Lord was published throughout all the region.*

Paul's expositions were so learned, so lucid, so filled with the very light of God that his message began to be talked about far and wide.

vv. 50 through 52

*But the Jews stirred up the devout and honourable women, and the chief men of the city, and raised persecution against Paul and Barnabas, and expelled them out of their coasts. But they shook off the dust of their feet against them, and came unto Iconium. And the disciples were filled with joy, and with the Holy Ghost.*

Wherever the whole truth of God in Christ is preached, some people always grow angry and begin to stir up trouble. If men are still running their own lives, confrontation with the truth of God can appear as an outright attack. They can become self-defensive, even violent. Here the full momentum of God through his Holy Spirit was active, so Paul and Barnabas were kicked out of the area. Did they leave depressed, feeling failures, certain they had let God down? Not at all. They shook the dust from their feet and went on to another town. And the holy hilarity of God possessed them as they went: "the disciples were filled with joy. . . ."

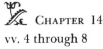 CHAPTER 14

vv. 4 through 8

*[In Iconium] the multitude of the city was divided: and part held with the Jews, and part with the apostles. And when there was an assault made both of the Gentiles, and also of the Jews with their rulers, to use them despitefully, and to stone them, They were ware of it, and fled unto Lystra and Derbe, cities of Lycaonia, and unto the region that lieth round about: And there they preached the gospel.*

One place was as good as another to these men. They had something to say! Creativity was upon them and within them.

vv. 8 through 11

*And there sat a certain man at Lystra, impotent in his feet, being a cripple from his mother's womb, who never had walked: The same heard Paul speak: who stedfastly beholding him, and perceiving that he had faith to be healed, Said with a loud voice, Stand upright on thy feet. And he leaped and walked. And when the people saw what Paul had done, they lifted up their voices, saying in the speech of Lycaonia, The gods are come down to us in the likeness of men.*

It is more than interesting that these Greek worshipers of pagan gods found it simple to believe their gods *could* come down to them in the likeness of men! No one taught them a "doctrine" that said Paul and Barnabas were "gods come down" as men. They found this the most logical thing to believe when they saw the healing. Why has it become so difficult for us to realize that God did a "natural," believable thing when he visited our earth in Jesus of Nazareth?

vv. 12 and 13

*And they called Barnabas, Jupiter; and Paul, Mercurius, because he was the chief speaker. Then the priest of Jupiter, which was before their city, brought oxen and garlands unto the gates, and would have done sacrifice with the people.*

Our society has done its best to gloss over man's deepest needs, but they are still just what they were then—including the need to worship.

vv. 14 through 18

*Which when the apostles, Barnabas and Paul, heard of, they rent their clothes, and ran in among the people, crying out, And saying, Sirs, why do ye these things? We also are men of like passions with you, and preach unto you that ye should turn from these vanities unto the living God, which made heaven, and earth, and the sea, and all things that are therein: Who in times past suffered all nations to walk in their own ways. Nevertheless he left not himself without witness, in that he did good, and gave us rain from heaven, and fruitful seasons, filling our hearts with food and gladness. And with these sayings scarce restrained they the people, that they had not done sacrifice unto them.*

Paul had a genius for speaking to people where they were. The only thing he attempted with those worshipers of many gods was to convince them that there was but one living God. He did not preach the death and Resurrection of Christ here. In his wisdom from God, he met these people with what they could understand. They were all set to worship him and Barnabas. His job at the moment was to turn them from this, and he did it by telling them of the goodness and love and mercy of the one God who, in spite of the history of nations going their own ways ignoring him, he "left not himself without witness." In his caring, God kept the rain falling and the fruit and grain growing and, in all the ways the people would permit, he filled their "hearts with food and gladness."

As with the gospel of Christ, even this much must have seemed too good to be true to Paul's pagan listeners. Also as with the gospel of Christ, though, it was too good not to be true. It stopped their attempted worship of Paul and Barnabas. Just barely, but it did stop it.

vv. 19 and 20

*And there came thither certain Jews from Antioch and Iconium, who persuaded the people, and, having stoned Paul, drew him out of the city, supposing he had been dead. Howbeit, as the disciples stood around about him, he rose up, and came into the city: and the next day he departed with Barnabas to Derbe.*

Paul must have been horribly injured. His enemies meant to kill him, and it isn't likely that they would have left their mission unfinished had they known he was not dead. After all, they had tracked him down at Lystra, from Antioch and Iconium. Still, the Spirit of life was so concentrated as the disciples stood around their fallen leader that "he rose up," went back into Lystra and was able to leave the next day for Derbe. This man, Paul, had been set in motion.

vv. 21 through 22

*And when they had preached the gospel to that city [Derbe], and had taught many, they returned again to Lystra, and to Iconium, and Antioch, Confirming the*

*souls of the disciples, and exhorting them to continue
in the faith, and that we must through much tribula-
tion enter into the kingdom of God.*

Paul was not only a man set in motion; he was a
man *enabled* by the Holy Spirit within him to move
about without fear—even back into the very towns of
Iconium and Antioch, the hometowns of the men who
traveled to Lystra to stone him to death. It was not
Paul's own "perfect love" which cast out his fear; it
was the love of God in him. This is a tremendous relief
and one which must be remembered when we are
afraid.

v. 23

*And when they had ordained them elders in every
church, and had prayed with fasting, they commended
them to the Lord, on whom they believed.*

Paul and Barnabas seem to have been practical men.
It is true that Paul, at times especially, was an eloquent
speaker, but he did not stop here. In every town where
they had won disciples to Christ, they handled the
business of forming the new churches for local rule
after they were gone. Both men did what they had to
do, but then had the humility to move on, commend-
ing the young church members "to the Lord, on whom
they believed."

vv. 24 through 26 and 28

*And after they had passed through Pisidia, they came
to Pamphylia. And when they had preached the word in
Perga, they went down into Attalia: And thence sailed*

*to Antioch, from whence they had been recommended*
*to the grace of God for the work which they fulfilled.*
*. . . And there they abode long time with the disciples.*

Paul and Barnabas had completed their first missionary journey. They were back again in Antioch where, so many miles and months and experiences ago, they had been waved off by the disciples. Now they stayed a long time with these disciples. When Paul was in action, he kept going, but I am impressed with his balance, especially in a man so intense and energetic and full of purpose. In spite of his intellect and seriousness of mind, he seemed, much of the time, to be a man almost driven by joy. And yet, now he was staying in Antioch to be a part of the new church there—to strengthen the others, but also to be strengthened by them. He was never a "traveling religioso" staying on the go, missing both the heartache and the inspiration of seeing people through their problems. To travel constantly is exhausting, but it is one thing to preach a sermon and move on. It is quite another thing to have the patience and wisdom to counsel and suffer with troubled people. Paul could do both.

 CHAPTER 15

v. 1

*And certain men which came down from Judaea*
*taught the brethren, and said, Except ye be circumcised*
*after the manner of Moses, ye cannot be saved.*

This was bound to happen sooner or later.

v. 2

*When therefore Paul and Barnabas had no small dis-
sension and disputation with them, they determined that
Paul and Barnabas, and certain other of them, should
go up to Jerusalem unto the apostles and elders about
this question.*

This, of course, was the first Christian Church
Conclave, and it is well, I think, to note that there
was a specific need for it. The young church, whatever
its faults, was at least not overorganized. When they
had a real problem, they got together to settle it. There
were no planned committee meetings or conventions
just because a date had come up on the calendar.

vv. 4 through 6

*And when they were come to Jerusalem, they were
received of the church, and of the apostles and elders,
and they declared all things that God had done with
them. But there rose up certain of the sect of the
Pharisees which believed, saying, That it was needful
to circumcise them, and to command them to keep the
law of Moses. And the apostles and elders came together
for to consider of this matter.*

There was really one matter and one only to decide
upon: Would Christianity break free of the laws of
Judaism and become a complete faith on its own, based
solely on confidence in the risen Lord, Jesus Christ?
Or would it remain a Jewish sect within the Mosaic

framework, made up of those who believed that the Messiah had come in Jesus, but who continued to obey the Law of Moses? Still more simply: Can a man be a Christian (whether he is Jew or Gentile) and not follow the Mosaic Law?

vv. 7 through 11

*And when there had been much disputing, Peter rose up, and said unto them, Men and brethren, ye know how that a good while ago God made choice among us, that the Gentiles by my mouth should hear the word of the gospel, and believe. And God, which knoweth the hearts, bare them witness, giving them the Holy Ghost, even as he did unto us; And put no difference between us and them, purifying their hearts by faith. Now therefore why tempt ye God, to put a yoke upon the neck of the disciples, which neither our fathers nor we were able to bear? But we believe that through the grace of the Lord Jesus Christ we shall be saved, even as they.*

Of course they disputed hotly, and of course Peter stood up. Even though much of the work among the Gentiles had been given to Paul by now, it had been Peter to whom the Lord gave the first hint of His love for Gentiles as well as Jews. No one could have been more shocked when the Spirit told him to go to the house of the Gentile Cornelius. But Peter went, and there he was convinced. A very high, ancient wall fell down for Peter that day as he stood among the members of Cornelius' family, seeing with his own eyes that God meant to include them too. He had been convinced once and for all, and so naturally he got up to speak now. And he spoke plainly, concisely, to the one point of trouble—either a man found salvation only through the grace of the Lord Jesus Christ, or he didn't. Peter knew for a fact that God "put no difference between us and them, purifying their hearts by faith." Not by obedience to this law and that—by faith.

v. 12

*Then all the multitude kept silence, and gave audience to Barnabas and Paul, declaring what miracles and wonders God had wrought among the Gentiles by them.*

Like Peter, Paul and Barnabas simply witnessed to what they had seen, experienced and knew to be fact. The evidence piled very high.

vv. 13, 19, 20 (Read vv. 13 through 20.)

*And after they had held their peace, James answered, saying, Men and brethren, hearken unto me: ... Wherefore my sentence is, that we trouble not them, which from among the Gentiles are turned to God: But that we write unto them, that they abstain from pollutions of idols, and from fornication, and from things strangled, and from blood.*

James, the head of the church at Jerusalem and Jesus' own brother, set the precedent. He quoted from the Old Testament and made a loving, inclusive, New Testament-tempered suggestion: Let us not trouble these Gentiles whose hearts have turned to

God. We will write them a letter giving them four rules to obey—and all of these four are for their good in the pagan society in which we Christians now live.

To some, it may seem that James was simply being expedient, forcing onto the Gentile believers just enough Judaism "to get by." This is not what he did at all. The four Christian abstinences were then beneficial ones, and they were, from that time on, to apply to Jewish Christians too.

vv. 22, 23, 30, 31

*Then pleased it the apostles and elders, with the whole church, to send chosen men of their own company to Antioch with Paul and Barnabas; namely, Judas surnamed Barsabas, and Silas, chief men among the brethren: And they wrote [sent] letters by them. . . . So when they were dismissed, they came to Antioch: and when they had gathered the multitude together, they delivered the epistle: Which when they had read, they rejoiced for the consolation.*

Indeed, it must have been a real "consolation." These Gentile Christians had been drawn to the faith by the Spirit of liberty, of love, of grace. They had become believers because of Jesus Christ. They had not been looking, within the context of Judaism, for a Messiah. They had been seeking the peace that comes from the forgiveness of their sins. That peace had come to them when they placed their faith in the resurrected Lord. His Resurrection was not a Jewish dogma to them—it was fact. Suddenly, to have been told by other legalistic Christians that they must now begin to obey certain laws in order to be saved must have distressed them deeply. Once all fears and anxieties had been stilled, Judas returned to Jerusalem, but Silas stayed in Antioch (verses 32–34). We are told that "it pleased Silas to abide there still." He must have had a particular affinity for these Gentiles who needed to learn now how to grow up in this new thoroughly *Christian* liberty.

vv. 35 and 36

> *Paul also and Barnabas continued in Antioch, teaching and preaching the word of the Lord, with many others also. And some days after Paul said unto Barnabas, Let us go again and visit our brethren in every city where we have preached the word of the Lord, and see how they do.*

Paul was not content with the "victories" of the first missionary journey. The "numbers" he and Barnabas reported back to the disciples and the Apostles did not content him. He wanted to "see how they do" by now. And this was no small, easily made decision. Travel in those days was difficult. There were ships when the routes could be covered by sea, but they were small, cramped, stocked with the bare necessities. Portions of the trip would be made on foot mile after mile along hot, dusty roads in constant danger of bandits who killed when they robbed. Paul was not suggesting a vacation from the church at Antioch. He was wholeheartedly about his Master's business. Jesus Christ

still filled Paul's horizons. Christ's concerns for the
new converts along the route of that first difficult
journey were Paul's too.

vv. 37 through 41

   *. . . Barnabas determined to take with them John,
   whose surname was Mark. But Paul thought not good
   to take him with them, who departed from them from
   Pamphylia, and went not with them to the work. And
   the contention was so sharp between them, that they
   departed asunder one from the other: and so Barnabas
   took Mark, and sailed unto Cyprus: And Paul chose
   Silas, and departed, being recommended by the brethren
   unto the grace of God. And he went through Syria and
   Cilicia, confirming the churches.*

This story has always been a heartbreak to me. After
what Paul and Barnabas had been through together—
after what they had accomplished as a team—to read
that the two Christian leaders contended so sharply
with each other that they separated is sad. Where was
God's will in this purely human dispute? Just where
it always is, on the side of love. God's love, of course,
since neither brother showed exactly what one could
call "love" toward the other. Still, each undoubtedly
had a point. After all, John Mark was Barnabas'
nephew. Barnabas felt a certain responsibility toward
him, I'm sure. And Paul was so intent upon a successful journey that he simply did not want a tempera-
mental young man along to add, perhaps, to the already
burdensome time ahead. Both men were probably

right in their decisions—even to separate. But the heartbreak comes with the words "the contention was so sharp between them." Evidently they separated in anger.

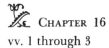 CHAPTER 16

vv. 1 through 3

*Then came he [Paul] to Derbe and Lystra: and, be-*
*hold, a certain disciple was there, named Timotheus, the*
*son of a certain woman, which was a Jewess, and be-*
*lieved; but his father was a Greek: Which was well*
*reported of by the brethren that were at Lystra and*
*Iconium. Him would Paul have to go forth with him;*
*and took and circumcised him because of the Jews*
*which were in those quarters: for they knew all that his*
*father was a Greek.*

In place of John Mark, Paul found "his son" Timothy, and here began one of the tenderest, closest relationships in the New Testament. Paul, as we have seen, because of his own clear light on the pure grace of God through Jesus Christ, was not a legalist. His obedience was strict, but it was motivated by love for the Lord Christ who, in spite of the disposition problems Paul might have had, did fill the Apostle's life. And so Paul did not circumcise Timothy from convictions of his own. He had seen too many works of grace among uncircumcised Gentiles by now ever to feel that circumcision was necessary, but he was using his balanced intelligence. Hundreds of Jews where he would be traveling with young Timothy knew the boy's father was a Greek. It would be best not to upset them unnecessarily—perhaps prevent their hearing a more important part of Paul's message.

vv. 8 through 10 (Read vv. 4 through 7.)

*And they passing by Mysia came down to Troas. And a vision appeared to Paul in the night; There stood a man of Macedonia, and prayed him, saying, Come over into Macedonia, and help us. And after he had seen the vision, immediately we endeavoured to go into Macedonia, assuredly gathering that the Lord had called us for to preach the gospel unto them.*

The first thing to notice here is that the narrator quite suddenly begins to use the first person pronoun. Since Luke is the author of the Acts of the Apostles, it is almost certain that the gentle, sensitive physician joined Paul's party at Troas, where the sea had stopped them temporarily. In verses 6 and 7, Paul's original plans to revisit the towns along the route of his first journey are changed at every turn. And at Troas, God redirected him in a most definite way—sending, for the first time, the message of Jesus Christ into Europe.

vv. 11 and 12

*Therefore loosing from Troas, we came with a straight course to Samothracia, and the next day to Neapolis; And from thence to Philippi, which is the chief city of that part of Macedonia . . . and we were in that city abiding certain days.*

Paul had done well on his first missionary journey, mainly to the Jews, but now God was centering down on His major purpose for His uniquely dedicated Apostle. He had to convince Paul through a vision, but at last the Christian gospel was to be heard on the continent of Europe. The momentous voyage took only a few days. The travelers—Paul, Timothy, Silas and now Luke, the doctor—landed at Neapolis and crossed the mountains to Philippi, ten miles away. On the plains of Philippi, nearly a century before, the fate of the world had been determined when Augustus and Antony had defeated Brutus and Cassius. Philippi was a military colony filled with sophisticated people— a miniature Rome. Paul and his friends saw there a clear picture of the moral and spiritual needs of the successful, cultivated citizens of their world. The people with whom they spent their time, both Greek and Jew, were not ordinary. Even the women of Philippi enjoyed privileges seldom experienced in the ancient East. Every citizen of Philippi was proud of both his city and his unique Roman privileges. God was seeking to show himself as he really is to the privileged class in Europe—and he had wisely chosen Paul.

vv. 13 through 15

*And on the sabbath we went out of the city by a river side, where prayer was wont to be made; and we sat down, and spake unto the women which resorted thither. And a certain woman named Lydia, a seller of purple, of*

*the city of Thyatira, which worshipped God, heard us:*
*whose heart the Lord opened, that she attended unto the*
*things which were spoken of Paul. And when she was*
*baptized, and her household, she besought us, saying, If*
*ye have judged me to be faithful to the Lord, come into*
*my house, and abide there. And she constrained us.*

I have always liked Lydia, although to me she seems
to be a little domineering. I know businesswomen like
Lydia—lovable, middle-aged, successful, their faces
showing the strain of having made it on their own—
and they are forever deciding just what other people
should do. Lydia was a successful businesswoman. She
dealt in the famous purple dye made from the secretion
of a native shellfish. Lydia had all she needed materi-
ally; evidently she had a large household. But her
heart was empty and, although she was a Gentile, she
had begun to join a small group of Jewish women by
the river for prayer. By the time Paul and his friends
reached Philippi, Lydia had come to believe in the
Lord God of the Jews. She was not a scoffer at religion.
She prayed; she worshiped God. And her heart was
so open that she seems to have been the first person
in the entire city to begin to believe Paul's message
about the risen Lord. Domineering, strong-minded
people are difficult to get along with at times; but when
they make up their minds, they act. Lydia did both.
She lost no time in being baptized and in seeing to it
that her entire household was baptized too, and then
she immediately "got Paul's guidance" for him! "If
you really believe I have become a Christian, then I

insist that you and your party move into my house to
live!" I think it's quite likely that they were already
comfortably settled elsewhere. Otherwise why would
Luke have emphasized that Lydia "besought"—persuaded—them? Finally she "constrained" them—gave
them no choice but to accept her enforced hospitality.
Those of you who, like me, live even a partially public
life know the type of hostess Lydia must have been.
But from Paul's first day in Europe her heart was
filled with the Spirit of Christ. If Lydia permitted it,
God would soon begin to melt away the rough edges
of her personality.

vv. 16 through 18

*And it came to pass, as we went to prayer, a certain
damsel possessed with a spirit of divination met us,
which brought her masters much gain by soothsaying:
The same followed Paul and us, and cried, saying, These
men are the servants of the most high God, which shew
unto us the way of salvation. And this did she many days.
But Paul, being grieved, turned and said to the spirit, I
command thee in the name of Jesus Christ to come out
of her. And he came out the same hour.*

I may be criticized for even intimating that not all
persons who have a "spirit of divination"—or who can
foresee future events—are evil people. I merely feel
that I am not the judge of these people. That many do
have certain powers of foretelling has long been a
proved fact. For years it has been, and still is, a subject
for calm, scientific, careful study at Duke University

and other schools. One thing seems certain here: This poor girl *could* both *see* and *foresee,* because she recognized Paul and Timothy and Silas and Luke as "servants of the most high God" and she knew not only that the people of Philippi had need of salvation, but that Paul and his friends could show them the way to find it.

What does seem equally apparent is that she *was* possessed of at least enough of the spirit of fear so that the men who were "making it big" by using her occult power were able to keep her chained to them in slavish obedience. Paul watched her pathetic tagging along, listened to her shrill, girlish voice shouting day after day; and when he could stand it no longer, he cast out the spirit which bound her to these men. I wish Luke had told us what happened to her after that. It is not likely that she changed her mind about Paul's message.

vv. 19 through 24

*And when her masters saw that the hope of their gains was gone, they caught Paul and Silas, and drew them into the marketplace unto the rulers, And brought them to the magistrates, saying, These men, being Jews, do exceedingly trouble our city, And teach customs, which are not lawful for us to receive, neither to observe, being Romans. And the multitude rose up together against them: and the magistrates rent off their clothes, and commanded to beat them. And when they had laid many stripes upon them, they cast them into prison, charging the jailor to keep them safely: Who, having received such a charge, thrust them into the inner prison, and made their feet fast in the stocks.*

Apparently Luke and Timothy were not jailed. Paul and Silas, I imagine, did all the preaching and teaching. There was no trial, and of course the charges were false. Both Paul and Silas were Roman citizens too, but they were given no chance to say so.

v. 25

*And at midnight Paul and Silas prayed, and sang praises unto God: and the [other] prisoners heard them.*

The two friends could not have been comfortable; their backs burned from the lashes which had been laid across them time and time again. There were no soothing ointments and no clean beds—only dried, caked blood and a damp stone floor. Their feet were chained to the wooden stocks, so that their stiff shoulders and backs could not even be rested by a shift in position. They had to sit up, their raw backs against a wall. But they praised God and sang songs! When we can sing while we suffer, someone is always going to "hear." When we can praise God after an unjust treatment of any kind, other "prisoners" will always "hear." The natural reaction under these circumstances would have been loud complaints and cursing. These men reacted *supernaturally*—they sang.

vv. 26 through 28

*And suddenly there was a great earthquake, so that the foundations of the prison were shaken: and immediately all the doors were opened, and every one's bands were loosed. And the keeper of the prison awaking*

*out of his sleep, and seeing the prison doors open, he*
*drew out his sword, and would have killed himself,*
*supposing that the prisoners had been fled. But Paul*
*cried with a loud voice, saying, Do thyself no harm: for*
*we are all here.*

Whether God sent the earthquake is beside the
point. Far more important is that he made such marvelous, creative, redemptive *use* of the quake (common in
that region) to bring about an even greater miracle
—the salvation of the jailer. At this point on my pilgrimage, above all things I see God as a redeemer—even
of such dreadful natural catastrophes as earthquakes.
He permitted it, of course, because deep within the
earth creation is continuing, but the quake merely gave
Paul a chance to *act like a Christian*. When God wanted
Peter out of jail, he sent a messenger, making it perfectly clear that Peter should leave. This time, God
*wanted* Paul and Silas to stay. And these two friends of
God knew him well enough to know this. They had not
been legally freed, and so Paul comforted the terrified
jailer, assuring him that they were all still there. Notice
that the other prisoners did not break and run either.
They had heard Paul and Silas singing praises to God
in the midst of their suffering. They found two men
they could trust, and so they did what Paul and Silas
did.

vv. 29 through 31

*Then he [the jailer] called for a light, and sprang in,*
*and came trembling, and fell down before Paul and*

*Silas, And brought them out, and said, Sirs, what must I do to be saved? And they said, Believe on the Lord Jesus Christ, and thou shalt be saved, and thy house.*

It *is* as simple as that. Why do we go on complicating God's magnificent simplicity?

vv. 32 through 34

*And they spake unto him the word of the Lord, and to all that were in his house. And he took them the same hour of the night, and washed their stripes; and was baptized, he and all his, straightway. And when he had brought them into his house, he set meat before them, and rejoiced, believing in God with all his house.*

The jailer was an abrupt, straightforward man. He entered the kingdom the same way—abruptly. God has no formula. He moves toward us at exactly the pace he knows we can accept. There is no doubt that the jailer was changed. His persecuting stopped at once, and he began to minister.

vv. 35 and 36

*And when it was day, the magistrates sent the serjeants, saying, Let those men go. And the keeper of the prison told this saying to Paul, The magistrates have sent to let you go: now therefore depart, and go in peace.*

After the ceremonies and the ministrations at the jailer's house during the night, Paul and Silas evidently went back to their cells. First thing the next morning, the jailer, wanting to show gratitude to his new brothers in Christ, used his "clout" with the magistrates to set his prisoners free.

vv. 37 through 39

*But Paul said unto them, They have beaten us openly uncondemned, being Romans, and have cast us into prison; and now do they thrust us out privily? nay verily; but let them come themselves and fetch us out. And the serjeants told these words unto the magistrates: and they feared, when they heard that they were Romans. And they came and besought them, and brought them out, and desired them to depart out of the city.*

Paul waited until just the right time to let it be known that he and Silas were Romans too. This is one of the many reasons God could send Paul among the Europeans.

v. 40

*And they went out of the prison, and entered into the house of Lydia: and when they had seen the brethren, they comforted them, and departed.*

The two friends walked out of the prison in dignity, escorted by the magistrates themselves; but before they left Philippi, they took time to call a meeting at Lydia's house for the encouragement of the members of the new Philippian church. What had happened to Paul and Silas did *not* depress them; rather, they were encouraged and emboldened by it.

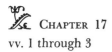 CHAPTER 17

vv. 1 through 3

*Now when they had passed through Amphipolis and Apollonia, they came to Thessalonica, where was a synagogue of the Jews: And Paul, as his manner was, went in unto them, and three sabbath days reasoned with them out of the scriptures. Opening and alleging, that Christ must needs have suffered, and risen again from the dead; and that this Jesus, whom I preach unto you, is Christ.*

There had not been enough Jews in Philippi for a synagogue, and so the handful had held their prayers by the river where Paul met Lydia. There was a synagogue in Thessalonica and, knowing full well what could happen eventually when the nonbelieving Jews in town learned that the Thessalonians were becoming Christians, Paul stood and preached Christ in sharp, definite, concise words. He left no doubt in anyone's mind that Jesus was the awaited Messiah. As Paul knew would happen, because he knew the drawing power of the Lord he followed, many Greek men and women began to follow the risen Jesus too (verse 4).

v. 5

*But the Jews which believed not, moved with envy, took unto them certain lewd fellows of the baser sort, and gathered a company, and set all the city on an uproar, and assaulted the house of Jason, and sought to bring them out to the people.*

". . . lewd fellows of the baser sort"—ne'er-do-wells —have not changed. They may still be "gathered" into "a company" for causing uproars in cities at the drop of the proverbial hat. It's human nature to relish disturbances in public—either as participants or observers. Mobs have not changed, but neither have the agitators who "gather a company." I do not speak of the cause here—merely of those who make the commotion, both behind the scenes and out front.

This mob, with no notion of why they were doing it, tracked Paul and Silas and Timothy and Luke down to the home of Jason, a believer, who had offered them his hospitality during their stay in Thessalonica. The members of the mob did not knock politely on the door, either. They "assaulted the house."

vv. 6 through 9

*And when they found them not, they drew Jason and certain brethren unto the rulers of the city, crying, These that have turned the world upside down are come hither also; Whom Jason hath received: and these all do contrary to the decrees of Caesar, saying that there is another king, one Jesus. And they troubled the people and the rulers of the city, when they heard these things. And when they had taken security of Jason, and of the other, they let them go.*

After all the trouble, the authorities ended up with only a little bail money from Jason and the other disciples. They did not find Paul and his friends. Of course,

Paul's work in Thessalonica was cut short, but one shining truth was uttered inadvertently by a Jew who helped drag Jason before the rulers of the city: "These that have turned the world upside down. . . ." The Spirit-filled Christians of the early Church were doing just that—in a redemptive way. Everything authentically Christian is looked at through the opposite end of the telescope from the view the world takes. Paul and his friends had learned so well how to rejoice in hardship—to make creative, redemptive use of every tragedy and every setback—that to those still in darkness they *must* have seemed to be living in an upside-down world.

vv. 10 through 15

*And the brethren immediately sent away Paul and Silas [apparently not Luke and Timothy] by night unto Berea . . . [where] many . . . believed; also of honourable women which were Greeks, and of men, not a few. But when the Jews of Thessalonica had knowledge that the word of God was preached of Paul at Berea, they came thither also, and stirred up the people. And then immediately the brethren sent away Paul to go as it were to the sea: but Silas and Timotheus abode there still. And they that conducted Paul brought him unto Athens: and receiving a commandment unto Silas and Timotheus for to come to him with all speed, they departed.*

Paul *had* truly been set in motion by the Spirit. One troubled time followed another, but his course was set. He was fighting "the good fight" and he knew it. Still,

Paul was quick to confess his own personal needs. Before he said good-bye to the Berean disciples who went with him as far as Athens, he asked them urgently to tell Timothy and Silas to come to him as quickly as possible. He needed them. His sufficiency in God left him free, as it always does, to need other people, as well as to be needed.

v. 16

*Now while Paul waited for them at Athens, his spirit was stirred in him, when he saw the city wholly given to idolatry.*

I can see the brilliant Apostle walking the wide streets of Athens—moving from one temple to another, from one altar to another; reading the inscriptions to pagan gods; turning to look at the Athenians strolling the wide streets in spiritual darkness, his weathered, sensitive face frowning; troubled to the depths of his heart. Paul knew the truth of eternal life in Christ—knew it well enough to be the leader in the new movement that was turning the world upside down. He knew Christ so well, loved him so wholly, that he could write in a later letter to his friends back in Philippi: "To me to live is Christ." Paul knew and with his fine mind sensed the spiritual hunger in these intellectually inclined Athenians—a hunger not met. And he grieved as he walked the streets of the beautiful city, waiting for his friends to join him.

v. 17

*Therefore disputed he in the synagogue with the Jews,
and with the devout persons, and in the market daily
with them that met with him.*

Paul had not been sent by the Spirit to Athens. He
was just waiting there for Silas and Timothy and Luke.
But so deeply was he troubled about the people of this
city filled with monuments and altars to pagan gods
that he simply could not restrain himself any longer.
He went first to the synagogue to discuss his faith with
devout Jews; and before he knew it, he was speaking
on the streets and in the marketplace—anywhere he
could get people to listen.

Of course, this was not the same then as with street-
corner preachers now. In Paul's time, this was the normal means of sharing ideas. There were no printed
books, no telephones or other electronic means of com-
munication. The wonder is not that he discussed Christ
with the men in the streets; the wonder is that, even
when he had this brief chance to rest, he couldn't. His
heart was so stirred toward the people.

vv. 18 through 21

*Then certain philosophers of the Epicureans, and of
the Stoicks, encountered him. And some said, What will
this babbler say? other some, He seemeth to be a setter
forth of strange gods: because he preached unto them
Jesus, and the resurrection. And they took him, and*

> brought him unto [the] Areopagus, saying, May we
> know what this new doctrine, whereof thou speakest,
> is? For thou bringest certain strange things to our ears:
> we would know therefore what these things mean. (For
> all the Athenians and strangers which were there spent
> their time in nothing else, but either to tell, or to hear
> some new thing.)

Paul's spirit was stirred toward these men, but his
intellect should have told him they were not really interested—only curious about what he believed. To
argue ideas, to listen to others, or to express one's own
theories constituted the most enjoyable kind of leisure
hours for the men of Athens. Perhaps Paul was too
weary to think clearly; perhaps by now he was moving
slightly toward the common trap of those whose profession is to win people to Jesus Christ. Perhaps Paul,
like so many faithful disciples now, had forgotten
how to be "just people." He just *had* to preach.

The Areopagus (City Council) met for some of its
sessions on Mars Hill. It met there when Paul stood up
that day.

vv. 22 and 23

> . . . Ye men of Athens, I perceive that in all things ye
> are too superstitious [very religious]. For as I passed by,
> and beheld your devotions, I found an altar with this
> inscription, TO THE UNKNOWN GOD. Whom there-
> fore ye ignorantly worship, him declare I unto you.

I wonder what might have happened if Paul had
either stopped here to permit their questions, or if he

had leaped from this loving, inclusive, sensitive intro-
duction into his clear statements about Christ. "I sense
your religious interest, gentlemen," he might have
said. "You are, by nature, religious people. As I walked
through your city, I even saw an altar which you have
inscribed TO THE UNKNOWN GOD. Men of
Athens, let me tell you his real name!"

But he didn't. I urge you to read Paul's speech to the
Athenians that day (verses 24 through 31). It is beauti-
fully worded. It shows Paul's broad knowledge of
Greco-Roman philosophy, poetry, sculpture, architec-
ture and religion. He brushed them all knowingly, de-
lighting the intellects of his hearers; but he touched
very few hearts, moved very few wills. As he went on
to Corinth, the zealous Apostle vowed never to speak
that way again. From that time on, he would "preach
Christ and him crucified." He would try with all his
heart to meet the real needs of his hearers, not merely
to titillate their minds. All that Paul said on Mars Hill
was true. He just didn't go far enough.

v. 33

*So Paul departed from among them.*

Timothy and Luke and Silas had not come yet, but
Paul left anyway—alone. I love him here in his partial
failure—his utter humanity—more than at any other
time.

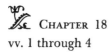 CHAPTER 18

vv. 1 through 4

*After these things Paul departed from Athens, and came to Corinth; And found a certain Jew named Aquila, born in Pontus, lately come from Italy, with his wife Priscilla; (because that Claudius had commanded all Jews to depart from Rome:) and came unto them. And because he was of the same craft, he abode with them, and wrought: for by their occupation they were tentmakers. And he reasoned in the synagogue every sabbath, and persuaded the Jews and the Greeks.*

This is a fascinating period in Paul's life. He had always been mainly a scholar. In those days scholars were supported by friends or relatives while they traveled and taught. Still, he did have a trade. Paul had, at some time in his life, been a tentmaker. And now, after his new resolve to preach Jesus Christ and him only, following the Mars Hill episode, he seems to be determined to simplify his daily life too. Something new seems to me to be stirring in Paul here. He needed, perhaps, a closer bond with people. Possibly he recognized his need for routine work for a while, for rest from the exhausting travel and preaching. Also, he must have been lonely. His friends had not yet been able to join him, and so he made two new friends—Aquila and Priscilla —who invited him to live in their home. On the sabbath, Paul could still continue his reasoning and preaching about Christ. This is a quieter, possibly deeper period for him in Corinth.

vv. 5 and 6

*And when Silas and Timotheus were come from Macedonia, Paul was pressed in the spirit, and testified to the Jews that Jesus was Christ. And when they opposed themselves, and blasphemed, he shook his raiment, and said unto them, Your blood be upon your own heads; I am clean: from henceforth I will go unto the Gentiles.*

By the time Timothy and Silas rejoined Paul in Corinth, he had dropped all nonessentials and was concentrating only upon preaching the one central truth —that the risen Jesus was the Christ, their Messiah. It is as though Paul were making one last effort to get through to his own people. He was down to bedrock. He had been working with his hands, perhaps spending more time alone, resting physically from his exhausting travels, and God had "centered him down" on the one absolute. I feel that in an entirely new way Christ was filling Paul's horizons. In spite of his new friends, Aquila and Priscilla, Paul must have felt lonely at times without Timothy and Silas. As he always does in the midst of loneliness if we let him, God became still more real to the Apostle. And when God grows more real to us, we invariably begin to drop the nonessentials. Everything becomes clarified. Decisions are simpler to make. Paul made his decision: He would stop trying to persuade his fellow Jews because they were paying no attention to him whatever. If he acted realistically (and this is what we do when God is central), he would simply stop trying and turn to the Gentiles. His conscience was free and clear. Paul's statement: "Your blood be upon your own heads; I am clean . . ." is translated in *Good News for Modern Man* as: "If you are lost, you yourselves must take the blame for it! I am not responsible." Such strong words show Paul's haunted mind where his own people were concerned. He loved them, he longed to see them living in the fulfillment of the Scriptural prophecies, but he came to the place where he felt that he had done all he could do. The Jews who did not accept Jesus as their Messiah were not evil people; they were just unteachable—too sure *they* were right. Their minds were closed.

vv. 7 and 8

*And he departed thence, and entered into a certain man's house, named Justus, one that worshipped God, whose house joined hard to the synagogue. And Crispus, the chief ruler of the synagogue, believed on the Lord with all his house; and many of the Corinthians hearing believed, and were baptized.*

Almost as soon as Paul decided to leave the Jews to their own fate, Crispus, a ruler of the synagogue, became a believer. Does this mean that Paul had made the wrong decision? I don't think so. What God is always trying to get us to do is to stay open—to keep his fresh air blowing through our minds. Paul may have needed to be reminded that Christ came for all people, not just Jews or just Gentiles. There are devout Christians today who seem to see need only among Jews or alcoholics or drug addicts or athletes or actors. Need is everywhere there is a human heart beating. We know this—even those who feel "called" to specialize in reaching one group or another—and yet our conditioning, our egos, our pride can get involved and God is the loser. Don't think for one minute that Paul had no pride, no ego operating overtime as our egos do. The great Apostle *was* an opinionated man. His mind was a good one; he respected his own thinking and was just as susceptible to getting his strong head confused with God's will as we are. Whether Paul made a right or a wrong decision when "he shook his raiment" at the Jews is not really relevant to what God seems to be saying in this incident. What appears to be important is that we are to stay open. Paul went right out and won a Jewish leader!

So many people exhaust themselves emotionally and spiritually by fretting over whether or not they have caught God's highest will in something. I've found that when I make my biggest mistakes, God sometimes makes his biggest gains—not only with me in the lessons I learn but, any time redemption is set free to operate, with everyone. God knows when we have made an honest mistake in judgment. If our error has been honestly made or innocently made or even ignorantly made, he goes immediately to work redeeming it.

vv. 9 through 11

*Then spake the Lord to Paul in the night by a vision,*
*Be not afraid, but speak, and hold not thy peace: For I*
*am with thee, and no man shall set on thee to hurt thee:*
*for I have much people in this city. And he continued*
*there a year and six months, teaching the word of God*
*among them.*

Even in the vision, God didn't clarify exactly
whether Paul had made the right decision. He just
reassured him and told him to go ahead without wasting
any time on perplexity or fear. Most of us want God
to be more specific. Nine times out of ten he won't be.
He loves us too much. If he were in the habit of putting
things down in black and white for us, we would de-
pend on that, and nothing could weaken faith more
surely. He said to Paul all Paul or anyone ever needs
to hear specifically: "Be not afraid . . . I am with thee."

vv. 12 through 17

*And when Gallio was the deputy of Achaia, the Jews*
*made insurrection with one accord against Paul, and*
*brought him to the judgment seat, Saying, This fellow*
*persuadeth men to worship God contrary to the law. And*
*when Paul was now about to open his mouth, Gallio*
*said unto the Jews, If it were a matter of wrong or*
*wicked lewdness, O ye Jews, reason would that I should*
*bear with you: But if it be a question of words and*
*names, and of your law, look ye to it; for I will be no*
*judge of such matters. And he drave them from the*
*judgment seat. Then all the Greeks took Sosthenes,*

*the chief ruler of the synagogue, and beat him before the*
*judgment seat. And Gallio cared for none of those things.*

Gallio has always interested me as a human being. He
would be a strong central character for a novel. Even
the exact date of Gallio's proconsularship is fixed now
by an inscription in Delphi which was discovered in
1905. Paul was dragged by the Jews before Gallio in
A.D. 52. Gallio, the brother of the philosopher Seneca,
who called him "sweet Gallio," must have been an at-
tractive, charming—certainly, a wise—ruler, the epi-
tome of religious tolerance. In fact, he was so just, so
quick to shut off the complaints of the nonbelieving
Jews, that he may have blocked God a little. It is quite
possible for God to use a nonbeliever to protect a
Christian as he used Gallio to set Paul free that day in
Corinth; but if Paul had been permitted to speak, some
might have believed. No one knows if this would have
happened, of course. At any rate, Gallio let Paul go and
made it possible for him to finish his Corinthian work
before he left for Syria with Priscilla and Aquila, to
begin what has come to be known as his third missionary journey (verse 18).

vv. 24 through 28 (Read vv. 19 through 23.)

*And a certain Jew named Apollos, born at Alexandria,*
*an eloquent man, and mighty in the scriptures, came to*
*Ephesus. This man was instructed in the way of the Lord;*
*and being fervent in the spirit, he spake and taught*
*diligently the things of the Lord, knowing only the*
*baptism of John. And he began to speak boldly in the*

*synagogue: whom when Aquila and Priscilla had heard,
they took him unto them, and expounded unto him the
way of God more perfectly. And when he was disposed
to pass into Achaia, the brethren wrote, exhorting the
disciples to receive him: who, when he was come, helped
them much which had believed through grace: For he
mightily convinced the Jews, and that publickly, shewing by the scriptures that Jesus was Christ.*

Apollos is a fascinating character too. Brilliant, eloquent, fervent, he must also have been an almost
uniquely humble man. Most leaders with followings
as large as those of Apollos would not have accepted
the teaching of two tentmakers. He did. Apollos had
all the truth except the one, central freeing fact of the
deity of Jesus Christ. When he had that, he was free
to be still greater.

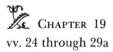 CHAPTER 19

vv. 24 through 29a

*For a certain man named Demetrius, a silversmith,
which made silver shrines for Diana, brought no small
gain unto the craftsmen; Whom he called together with
the workmen of like occupation, and said, Sirs, ye know
that by this craft we have our wealth. Moreover ye see
and hear, that not alone [here] at Ephesus, but almost
throughout all Asia, this Paul hath persuaded and turned
away much people, saying that they be no gods, which
are made with hands: So that not only this our craft is
in danger . . . but . . . the temple of the great goddess
Diana. . . . And when they heard these sayings, they*

*were full of wrath, and cried out saying, Great is Diana of the Ephesians. And the whole city was filled with confusion. . . .*

There is never a letdown in the genuine drama of the Acts of the Apostles. Wherever Paul went, conflict inevitably resulted—not because he tried to stir it up, but because he held up Jesus Christ and man slammed himself invariably against His purity. In Ephesus, after long months of success, Paul was caught again between the evil of man and the purity of Christ—at the point where the drama takes place. Here, the Apostle stood to hurt business. A riot resulted. There isn't always the noisy melodrama of the outbreak in the temple at Ephesus. More often the truth of Christ causes inner rebellion, but there is the drama just the same; and there always will be when man's selfish motives smash against the pure heart of Christ.

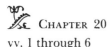 CHAPTER 20

vv. 1 through 6

*And after the uproar [in Ephesus] was ceased, Paul called unto him the disciples, and embraced them, and departed for to go into Macedonia. And when he had gone over those parts, and had given them much exhortation, he came into Greece. And there abode three months. And when the Jews laid wait for him, as he was about to sail into Syria, he purposed to return through Macedonia. And there accompanied him into Asia Sopater of Berea; and of the Thessalonians, Aristarchus and Secundus; and Gaius of Derbe, and Timotheus; and of Asia, Tychicus and Trophimus. These going before tarried for us at Troas.*

In verse 6, Luke lets us know that he rejoined Paul on the journey. In his absence, Luke has reported by way of research and interviews with those who were with Paul—probably interviews with Paul himself. From this point on, there is far more detail. Luke is seeing it all happen firsthand.

vv. 7 through 10

*And upon the first day of the week, when the disciples came together to break bread, Paul preached unto them, ready to depart on the morrow; and continued his speech until midnight. And there were many lights in the upper chamber, where they were gathered together. And there sat in a window a certain young man named Eutychus, being fallen into a deep sleep: and as Paul was long preaching, he sunk down with sleep, and fell down from the third loft, and was taken up dead. And Paul went down, and fell on him, and embracing him said, Trouble not yourselves; for his life is in him.*

In a daily devotional book* I once wrote:

What might have happened had Paul been insulted at the boy's falling asleep in the middle of his lengthy sermon? God would still have had the power to bring the

---

* *Share My Pleasant Stones* (Grand Rapids: Zondervan Publishing House, 1957).

boy to life, but could that power have gotten through Paul if he had been suddenly filled up with wounded pride? A tragedy might have been left a tragedy.

Paul evidently wasn't insulted and, instead of ending in tragedy and turmoil, the meeting ended in joy. The Apostle even went back upstairs and finished his sermon, talking until daybreak (verse 11).

v. 16

*For Paul had determined to sail by Ephesus, because he would not spend the time in Asia: for he hasted, if it were possible for him, to be at Jerusalem the day of Pentecost.*

One is reminded here of Jesus' determination to take one and then another step along the way to Jerusalem. Paul knew, as his Master had known, that the ultimate trial could come there. All through the third missionary journey, his enemies among the Jews had plagued him. He had no reason to think he might escape them in the Holy City, and yet he pushed on. For months he had been carrying money from the other churches for the mother church in Jerusalem. Paul wanted to deliver the gifts at Pentecost.

vv. 22 and 23 (Read vv. 17 through 21.)

*And now, behold, I go bound in the spirit unto Jerusalem, not knowing the things that shall befall me there: Save that the Holy Ghost witnesseth in every city, saying that bonds and afflictions abide me.*

In Miletus, after having called the faithful believers from Ephesus to meet with him, Paul makes no effort to hide either his Christian tenderness and concern for them or his sure knowledge that trouble lies ahead.

v. 24

*But none of these things move me, neither count I my life dear unto myself, so that I might finish my course with joy, and the ministry, which I have received of the Lord Jesus, to testify the gospel of the grace of God.*

Aside from his line from the Philippian letter in which Paul wrote "To me to live is Christ," the first line of verse 24 is for me the most important in all the Pauline literature: "none of these things move me. . . ." Perhaps, if we are honest, this testimony of Paul's inner steadiness, if it has released us at all, has released us from some form of fear. We fear death, the death of a loved one—the grief and empty hours that follow. We fear criticism, the sting of it, the anxiety from it. We fear failure and illness and loneliness. We fear for our jobs, for our old age. We fear depending on someone other than ourselves. We fear not being liked. At the bottom of most of our troubles lies some kind of fear. Paul was not saying that he was full of courage and fearless. He simply said, in effect, that whatever lay ahead, none of it would change his love for Jesus Christ. He would not be moved from living by that love.

I used to fear criticism from God's people. I don't any more, and Paul has helped me enormously. When he began to speak to the Ephesians at this last sad fare-well, he said (verse 18) : "Ye know, from the first day that I came into Asia, after what manner I have been with you at all seasons." Paul had made mistakes and hasty judgments, as we do, but they knew his life. He had kept his accounts clear with God. If being his best self in Christ was going to bring down persecution when he reached Jerusalem, so be it. "None of these things move me." We will always feel fears—I'm sure Paul did. But no matter what happens, we need not be "moved" from our course. If we have "fought the good fight" as he felt he had, we need not be unduly moved by trouble up ahead. After all, trouble is up ahead for everyone. No one escapes. It is clear that Paul was not seeking sympathy from the Ephesians gathered around him to say good-bye. Nor was he seeking to appear spiritual. He was merely stating a fact. And perhaps a clue to the way he achieved this kind of inner calm "in the midst of" lies in his use of the word "joy" instead of courage or bravery. "But none of these things move me, neither count I my life dear unto myself, so that I might finish my course with joy. . . ." As Oswald Chambers once said, "Joy is God in your blood." No amount of trouble can rob a Christian of the joy Jesus left us.

v. 32 (Read vv. 25 through 31.)

*And now, brethren, I commend you to God, and to the word of his grace, which is able to build you up, and to give you an inheritance among all them which are sanctified.*

Only God is able to "build us up" through grace. I have yet to learn an adequate definition of grace, but I have learned the hard way that only grace can add to my inner being. If only we could begin to see the difference between self-effort in God's behalf and cooperation with him as he does the work in us!

vv. 36 through 38

*And when he had thus spoken, he kneeled down, and prayed with them all. And they all wept sore, and fell on Paul's neck, and kissed him. Sorrowing most of all for the words which he spake, that they should see his face no more. And they accompanied him unto the ship.*

Little needs to be said here, except that these early Christians were not afraid to express their feelings of genuine affection. What would we say now if two Christian men wept and kissed each other good-bye?

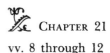 CHAPTER 21

vv. 8 through 12

*And the next day we that were of Paul's company departed, and came unto Caesarea: and we entered into the house of Philip the evangelist, which was one of the seven; and abode with him. And the same man had four daughters, virgins, which did prophesy. And as we tarried there many days, there came down from Judaea a certain prophet, named Agabus. And when he was come unto us, he took Paul's girdle, and bound his own hands and feet, and said, Thus saith the Holy Ghost, So shall the Jews at Jerusalem bind the man that owneth this girdle, and shall deliver him into the hands of the Gentiles. And when we heard these things, both we, and they of that place, besought him [Paul] not to go up to Jerusalem.*

Paul was not going to be taken by surprise in Jerusalem. The Holy Spirit was seeing to that. The disciples in Tyre (though the Spirit) had warned him. Here was another graphic warning. I do not think that God gave Paul all these definite warnings so much for Paul's sake as for the sake of the people to whom Paul spoke along the way. By this time, one warning to the faithful Apostle would have been enough. God knew this. The repeated warnings must have been so that Paul would have a chance every place he stopped to *demonstrate* —by his words as well as by his steady demeanor—that "none of these things moved" him.

vv. 13 through 15

*Then Paul answered, What mean ye to weep and to break mine heart? for I am ready not to be bound only, but also to die at Jerusalem for the name of the Lord Jesus. And when he would not be persuaded, we ceased, saying, The will of the Lord be done. And after those days we took up our carriages, and went up to Jerusalem.*

The disciples (Luke among them) tried everything. When Paul would not turn back from Jerusalem, they turned the whole problem over to God. Paul had done it long before that.

vv. 18 through 22

*And the day following Paul went in with us unto James; and all the elders were present. And when he . . . declared particularly what things God had wrought among the Gentiles by his ministry . . . they glorified the Lord, and said unto him [Paul], Thou seest, brother, how many thousands of Jews there are which believe; and they are all zealous of the law: And they are informed of thee, that thou teachest all the Jews which are among the Gentiles to forsake Moses, saying that they ought not to circumcise their children, neither to walk after the customs. What is it therefore? the multitude must needs come together: for they will hear that thou art come.*

Paul had been in the field so long—had lived the life of liberty in Christ away from the organized church, watching the direct work of the Holy Spirit— that he may have forgotten the feel of the restrictions of the mother church in Jerusalem. If he had forgotten, by this time in James' little speech it had all come back to him. But Paul had been truly liberated—he was free from within where it counted. Whatever James had to say, he could meet the request in love. He waited quietly, and James went on.

vv. 23 and 24

*Do therefore this that we say to thee: We have four men which have a vow on them; Them take, and purify thyself with them, and be at charges with them, that they may shave their heads: and all may know that those things, whereof they were informed concerning thee, are nothing; but that thou thyself also walkest orderly, and keepest the law.*

Paul was free of the law in Christ, but he was not outside it, as Christ was not. Jerusalem would be thronging with people. It was the Jewish Feast of Pentecost. No one knew better than Paul how he had been criticized by the unbelieving Jews. The brethren in the Jerusalem church were right. He would not be acting in love if he refused to do what he could to keep peace and harmony in the church. The Nazarite vow he had been asked to take required four weeks, but a man who had purified himself could attach himself to three other men already entered into the rituals of the vow. The Christian Jewish brothers in Jerusalem had anticipated the need for Paul to make some outward show that he was still orthodox in order to quiet the gossip of the Jews who had not accepted Christ. Three men had already made the Nazarite observance for three weeks. Seven days remained.

vv. 26 through 28

*Then Paul took the men, and the next day purifying himself with them entered into the temple, to signify the accomplishment of the days of purification, until that an offering should be offered for every one of them. And when the seven days were almost ended, the Jews which were of Asia, when they saw him in the temple, stirred up all the people, and laid hands on him, Crying out, Men of Israel, help: This is the man, that teacheth*

> *. . . against the people, and the law, and this place: and*
> *[has] further brought Greeks also into the temple, and*
> *hath polluted this holy place.*

Paul's attempt to pacify his critics did not work.
The non-Christian Jews who had come to Jerusalem
for Pentecost from Asia were already convinced of
Paul's lack of orthodoxy. Nothing he could have done
would have changed their attitude toward him. They
had seen him with Greeks in Asia (verse 29), and
that's what they "saw" in Jerusalem.

vv. 30 through 36

> *And all the city was moved, and the people ran to-*
> *gether: and they took Paul, and drew him out of the*
> *temple: and forthwith the doors were shut. And as they*
> *went about to kill him, tidings came unto the chief*
> *captain of the band, that all Jerusalem was in an uproar.*
> *Who immediately took soldiers and centurions, and ran*
> *down unto them: and . . . they left beating of Paul. Then*
> *the chief captain . . . took him, and commanded him to*
> *be bound with two chains; and demanded who he was,*
> *and what he had done. And some cried one thing, some*
> *another, among the multitude: and when he [the captain]*
> *could not know the certainty for the tumult, he com-*
> *manded him [Paul] to be carried into the castle. . . . the*
> *multitude of the people followed after, crying, Away*
> *with him.*

A not too distant echo must have rung in Paul's
ears: Crucify him! Crucify him! Like his Master, Paul

had been judged by what the people chose to think of him—not for what he was. In the midst of an act of love toward his Jewish persecutors, God permitted Paul to be attacked and beaten. The Apostle was trying to make a bridge to the Jews, and seemingly his effort had failed. But had it? God's ultimate purpose is always love, but he knew he could trust Paul to allow him to include even Paul's enemies in that love. If they had not tried to kill Paul, his ritual of love in the temple might have gone unnoticed. God did not prompt the attack; he *used* it. He did not protect Paul because He needed him to be as He knew Paul would be in the midst of suffering and attack.

vv. 37, 39, 40a

> *And as Paul was to be led into the castle, he said unto the chief captain, May I speak unto thee? Who said, Canst thou speak Greek? . . . [And] Paul said, I am a man which am a Jew of Tarsus, a city in Cilicia, a citizen of no mean city: and, I beseech thee, suffer me to speak unto the people. And when he had given him licence, Paul stood on the stairs, and beckoned with the hand unto the people.*

By now Paul knew God's ways. Paul was ready to let Him work through his suffering in order to reach the people who hated him, but whom he knew God loved. Standing on the palace stairs, Paul, bound by two chains, his back and face bleeding from the beating, began to speak to the people in Hebrew.

 CHAPTER 22

vv. 1 through 3

*Men, brethren, and fathers, hear ye my defence which I make now unto you. (And when they heard that he spake in the Hebrew tongue to them, they kept the more silence: and he saith,) I am verily a man which am a Jew, born in Tarsus, a city in Cilicia, yet brought up in this city at the feet of Gamaliel, and taught according to the perfect manner of the law of the fathers, and was zealous toward God, as ye all are this day.*

With all his being, Paul is trying to identify with his listeners, by speaking in their Hebrew tongue and by assuring them that, in spite of their drastic differences, he knows they too are "zealous toward God."

v. 4

*And I persecuted this way unto the death, binding and delivering into prisons both men and women.*

"And I persecuted *this way*." Paul may have gestured toward his own wounds and chains as he struggled to let them know that he knew how they felt toward him. He had done to other Christians what they were doing to him now.

vv. 5 through 8

*As also the high priest doth bear me witness, and all the estate of the elders: from whom also I received letters unto the brethren, and went to Damascus, to*

*bring them which were there bound unto Jerusalem, for
to be punished. And it came to pass, that, as I . . . was
come nigh unto Damascus about noon, suddenly there
shone from heaven a great light round about me. And I
fell unto the ground, and heard a voice saying unto me,
Saul, Saul, why persecutest thou me? And I answered,
Who art thou, Lord? And he said unto me, I am Jesus
of Nazareth, whom thou persecutest.*

Apparently, even the mention of the hated name of
Jesus did not break the attentiveness of Paul's audience.
After all, this was a highly dramatic story and the
Apostle was a dynamic speaker. He still had their at-
tention.

vv. 9 through 11

*And they that were with me saw indeed the light, and
were afraid; but they heard not the voice of him that
spake to me. And I said, What shall I do, Lord? And the
Lord said unto me, Arise, and go into Damascus; and
there it shall be told thee of all things which are appointed for thee to do. And when I could not see for the
glory of that light, being led by the hand of them that
were with me, I came into Damascus.*

Paul did not say that he was blind. He said he could
not see "for the glory of that light." So real was his
encounter with the living Jesus Christ that day on the
Damascus road that even sudden blindness was like
a great light. Paul's very being was so filled with the
"glory of that light" that the fact he had to be led by
the hand would have seemed secondary.

vv.12 through 14

*And one Ananias, a devout man according to the law, having a good report of all the Jews which dwelt there, Came unto me, and stood, and said unto me, Brother Saul, receive thy sight. And the same hour I looked up upon him. And he said, The God of our fathers hath chosen thee, that thou shouldest know his will, and see that Just One, and shouldest hear the voice of his mouth. For thou shalt be his witness unto all men of what thou hast seen and heard.*

As Paul spoke from the palace stairs in chains, he was *being* the "voice of his mouth." He used no embellishments. He was not preaching a sermon. What he had to say was a simple, unadorned witness to the God of their fathers. "I met that God on the road to Damascus that day," he was saying, "and He changed me."

vv. 16 through 18

*And now [Ananias said] why tarriest thou? arise, and be baptized, and wash away thy sins, calling on the name of the Lord. And it came to pass, that, when I was come again to Jerusalem, even while I prayed in the temple, I was in a trance; And saw him saying unto me, Make haste, and get thee quickly out of Jerusalem: for they will not receive thy testimony concerning me.*

Still the Jews in Paul's audience did not begin to shout. Even with this reference to them, they held their silence.

vv. 19 through 22

*And I said, Lord, they know that I imprisoned and
beat in every synagogue them that believed on thee:
And when the blood of thy martyr Stephen was shed, I
also was standing by, and consenting unto his death, and
kept the raiment of them that slew him. And he said
unto me, Depart: for I will send thee far hence unto the
Gentiles. And they gave him audience unto this word,
and then lifted up their voices, and said, Away with such
a fellow from the earth: for it is not fit that he should
live.*

"And they gave him audience unto this word":
*Gentiles.* Somehow Paul had held the Jews through
his clear, unmistakable witness to Jesus Christ as the
Messiah. He had crossed their theological beliefs and
they listened without interrupting him; but when he
spoke the word "Gentiles," bedlam broke out. The
Jews would do business with the Gentiles, would even
obey their government officials up to a point; but it
must be remembered that to be a Jew in those days
meant far more to the Jew than merely having someone agree with him theologically. To have been born
a Jew was to have been born privileged, chosen of
God. Their hatred of Paul's insistence that God included Gentiles in his love and his redemptive plan
raised more than a doctrinal issue; it was also a red-hot
social issue. Gentiles were unclean people. Gentiles
were inferior people. Jews would neither worship nor

eat with them. Even Gentile dishes were unclean. Does
this sound familiar? These Jews were respectable,
cultivated, educated. But they were convinced of their
superiority to Gentiles, and even Paul's straightforward witness to the all-inclusive love of God could not
sway them. He raised the one social issue that raised
hackles, as it does among some now when integration
of the races is mentioned. To the angered Jews who
heard Paul that day, Gentiles were all right—in their
places. In the marketplace, on the streets, but not at
Jewish tables or in the Jewish temple. Recently I spoke
in churches and at luncheons and dinners from Cali-
fornia to South Carolina and not one black face did I
see. I missed them. So did God. Bedlam broke loose
when Paul said the unacceptable word: Gentiles.

vv. 23 through 25

*And as they cried out, and cast off their clothes, and
threw dust into the air, The chief captain commanded
him to be brought into the castle, and bade that he
should be examined by scourging; that he [the captain]
might know wherefore they cried so against him. And
as they bound him with thongs, Paul said unto the
centurion that stood by, Is it lawful for you to scourge
a man that is a Roman, and uncondemned?*

God had a steady disciple in Paul. Not once during
all the maltreatment did the Apostle stop using his
Spirit-enlightened mind. It is no wonder he wrote
that we are to "let this mind be in you which was in

Christ Jesus." Paul could write that. He had "let" that mind invade his.

vv. 26 through 30

*When the centurion heard that [Paul's question], he went and told the chief captain, Take heed . . . this man is a Roman. Then the chief captain came, and said unto him [Paul], Tell me, art thou a Roman? He said, Yea. And the chief captain answered, With a great sum obtained I this freedom [this Roman citizenship]. And Paul said, But I was free born. Then straightway they departed from him . . . and the chief captain also was afraid. . . . On the morrow, because he would have known the certainty wherefore he [Paul] was accused of the Jews, he loosed him from his bands, and commanded the chief priests and all their council to appear, and brought Paul down, and set him before them.*

Paul knew the law as intimately as he knew grace. And as he was led before the council, which he knew to be made up of both Pharisees and Sadducees, he was on familiar ground. He must have welcomed still another chance to witness as he stood up to speak in his own defense before these rulers.

 CHAPTER 23

vv. 1 and 2

*And Paul, earnestly beholding the council, said, Men and brethren, I have lived in all good conscience before God until this day. And the high priest Ananias com-*

*manded them that stood by him to smite him on the mouth.*

Paul found less courtesy with the rulers than he had found with the angry mob the day before.

vv. 3 through 5

*Then said Paul unto him, God shall smite thee, thou whited wall: for sittest thou to judge me after the law, and commandest me to be smitten contrary to the law? And they that stood by said, Revilest thou God's high priest? Then said Paul, I wist not, brethren, that he was the high priest: for it is written, Thou shalt not speak evil of the ruler of thy people.*

The blow on the mouth must have startled Paul. After all, he was just beginning his defense. He had spoken only one sentence. The great Apostle was human. A sudden blow can bring a quick, spiteful reaction from anyone. Paul lashed out, but as quickly recanted when he realized that he had been caustic with the high priest himself. His Christianity came to the fore, even to quoting the Scripture that proved him wrong to have said what he said to Ananias.

vv. 6 through 10

*But when Paul perceived that the one part were Sadducees, and the other Pharisees, he cried out in the council, Men and brethren, I am a Pharisee, the son of a Pharisee: of the hope and resurrection of the dead I am called in question. And when he had so said, there arose a dissension between the Pharisees and the Sad-*

*ducees: and the multitude was divided. For the Sad-
ducees say that there is no resurrection, neither angel,
nor spirit: but the Pharisees confess both. And there
arose a great cry . . . and . . . a great dissension, [and] the
chief captain, fearing lest Paul should have been pulled
in pieces of them, commanded the soldiers to go down,
and to take him by force from among them, and to
bring him into the castle.*

Wise Paul merely used a bit of psychology here—
and it worked.

v. 11

*And the night following the Lord stood by him, and
said, Be of good cheer, Paul: for as thou hast testified
of me in Jerusalem, so must thou bear witness also at
Rome.*

God always knows when, in spite of the fact that we
may appear to be doing rather well, we need further
reassurance. He not only came to Paul that night in
prison; he added comfort by calling the harassed disciple by his name. "Be of good cheer, Paul."

v. 12

*And when it was day, certain of the Jews banded to-
gether, and bound themselves under a curse, saying that
they would neither eat nor drink till they had killed
Paul.*

The pure life of Christ within Paul was driving his
enemies to further deeds of evil just as surely as Christ's
life drove His enemies a few years before.

v. 16

*And when Paul's sister's son heard of their lying in*
*wait, he went and entered into the castle, and told Paul.*

Nothing has been said before and nothing is said
following this incident of Paul's nephew. We aren't
even told the boy's name, but God obviously used the
young man to save his uncle's life.

vv. 17 through 22

*Then Paul called one of the centurions unto him,*
*and said, Bring this young man unto the chief captain:*
*for he hath a certain thing to tell him. So he took him.*
. . . *[And] the chief captain took him by the hand, and*
*went with him aside privately, and asked him, What is*
*that thou hast to tell me? And he said, The Jews have*
*agreed to desire thee that thou wouldest bring down Paul*
*to morrow into the council, as though they would en-*
*quire somewhat of him more perfectly. But do not thou*
*yield unto them: for there lie in wait for him of them*
*more than forty men, which have bound themselves*
*with an oath, that they will neither eat nor drink till*
*they have killed him: and now are they ready, looking*
*for a promise from thee. So the chief captain then let*
*the young man depart, and charged him, See thou tell*
*no man that thou hast shewed these things to me.*

We are told so little—almost nothing of Paul's
family—but even without a known name, this young
man stands out. He must have shown genuine integrity,

or the chief captain would not have trusted his story. The boy impressed the chief captain because he lost no time in acting.

vv. 23 and 24

*And he called unto him two centurions, saying, Make ready two hundred soldiers to go to Caesarea, and horsemen threescore and ten, and spearmen two hundred, at the third hour of the night; And provide them beasts, that they may set Paul on, and bring him safe unto Felix the governor.*

The chief captain, whose name we now know to be Claudius Lysius (verse 26), saw to it that Paul arrived in Caesarea safely and swiftly. God meant it when He told Paul he would have a chance to witness in Rome also. He was on his way. A letter of explanation of Paul's predicament accompanied him, written by Claudius Lysius to Felix, the Caesarean governor. (Read verses 26 through 30.) The letter's tone implies that Claudius had come to believe Paul's innocence of the nebulous charges.

vv. 33 through 35

*Who, when they came to Caesarea, and delivered the epistle to the governor, presented Paul also before him. And when the governor had read the letter, he asked of what province he was. And when he understood that he was of Cilicia; I will hear thee, said he, when thine accusers are also come. And he commanded him to be kept in Herod's judgment hall.*

Paul's thoughts as he waited in Herod's judgment hall—still a prisoner in chains—must have been anxious ones. He knew that the Jews who refused the Messiah he proclaimed would come prepared. They were well able to afford the best legal counsel. They would have it. The wait must have seemed long indeed.

 CHAPTER 24

vv. 1 and 5 through 9

*And after five days Ananias the high priest descended with the elders, and with a certain orator named Tertullus, who informed the governor against Paul. . . . For we have found this man a pestilent fellow, and a mover of sedition among all the Jews throughout the world, and a ringleader of the sect of the Nazarenes: Who also hath gone about to profane the temple: whom we took, and would have judged according to our law. But the chief captain Lysias came upon us, and with great violence took him away out of our hands, Commanding his accusers to come unto thee. . . . And the Jews also assented, saying that these things were so.*

The old boys really meant to silence Paul one way or another. The journey from Jerusalem to Caesarea was sixty-four long miles, but they did not rest at merely having Paul out of Jerusalem. They wanted him dead. Even the high priest Ananias came along.

vv. 10 through 13 and 21

*Then Paul, after that the governor had beckoned unto him to speak, answered, Forasmuch as I know that*

*thou hast been of many years a judge unto this nation,
I do the more cheerfully answer for myself: Because that
thou mayest understand, that there are yet but twelve
days since I went up to Jerusalem for to worship. And
they neither found me in the temple disputing with any
man, neither raising up the people, neither in the synagogues, nor in the city: Neither can they prove the
things whereof they now accuse me. . . . Except it be
for this one voice, that I cried standing among them,
Touching the resurrection of the dead I am called in
question by you this day.*

Paul minced no words. Categorically, he denied all
their accusations as stated by their lawyer, Tertullus,
but added that he was "guilty" of believing in the
resurrection of the dead. Once more, Paul turned a
defense into a witness.

vv. 22, 23

*And when Felix heard these things, having more per-
fect knowledge of that way, he deferred them, and said,
When Lysias the chief captain shall come down, I will
know the uttermost of your matter. And he commanded
a centurion to keep Paul, and to let him have liberty,
and that he should forbid none of his acquaintance to
minister or come unto him.*

Felix passed the buck—at least in part. His decision
was to keep Paul a prisoner, but with many liberties,
even visits by his friends. There is no indication that
Felix sent for Lysius to come down to Caesarea. Somehow the governor had been exposed to The Way of the

early Christians and, although he didn't have the courage to free Paul for fear of more trouble from the
Jews, he imprisoned him as lightly as possible. He
seemed more interested in the quick departure of
Paul's accusers than in justice. Felix was not anti-
Christian or pro-Christian. He was merely being expedient.

vv. 24 through 26

*And after certain days, when Felix came with his wife
Drusilla, which was a Jewess, he sent for Paul, and heard
him concerning the faith in Christ. And as he reasoned
of righteousness, temperance, and judgment to come,
Felix trembled, and answered, Go thy way for this time;
when I have a convenient season, I will call for thee.
He hoped also that money should have been given him
of Paul, that he might loose him: wherefore he sent for
him the oftener, and communed with him.*

I have heard sermons on this passage telling of Felix'
relationship with Paul which argued that Felix was
near the kingdom—the point of the sermons being
that no one should put God off until a more "convenient season." I doubt that we can really know about
Felix, the governor of the sophisticated city of Caesarea.
Furthermore, I doubt that Felix knew all his own
motives in taking his wife, Drusilla, to hear Paul speak
about Christ. I'm sure Felix was hoping for a bribe
from Paul, and this explains the frequency of the visits
the governor permitted Paul to make to his quarters.
Felix did tremble when Paul spoke of "righteousness,

temperance, and judgment to come"—and it is, of course, altogether possible that Felix was both expedient *and* "under conviction" as the old-fashioned preachers said. We are like this as human beings. Our motives are almost always mixed.

v. 27

> But after two years Porcius Festus came into Felix' room: and Felix, willing to shew the Jews a pleasure, left Paul bound.

Felix' ultimate recorded act when he left office was pure expediency. Two years in semiconfinement is a long time. The added wait must have been the most difficult of all for Paul.

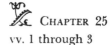 CHAPTER 25

vv. 1 through 3

> Now when Festus was come into the province, after three days he ascended from Caesarea to Jerusalem. Then the high priest and the chief of the Jews informed him against Paul, and besought him, And desired favour against him, that he would send for him to Jerusalem, laying wait in the way to kill him.

Poor old hate-filled men! Two years had passed since they had appeared before Felix in an effort "to get" Paul, and still they were hard at it. What is it about hate that often seems to cause it to outlast love? Is it because hate feeds the human ego—turns one in

on oneself—while love, if it is real love, always turns
outward toward the loved one?

vv. 4 and 5

*But Festus answered, that Paul should be kept at
Caesarea, and that he himself would depart shortly
thither. Let them therefore, said he, which among you
are able, go down with me, and accuse this man, if there
be any wickedness in him.*

I feel now like saying "Poor Festus." Here is another
Roman governor caught in the squeeze of Paul's righteousness and the hatred of his enemies. Every Roman
ruler wanted to please the Jews enough to keep peace
but, as with Felix, Festus couldn't have cared less about
their Law—or Paul. He was simply in the same political
bind in which Felix served out his term as governor.

v. 11

*For if I be an offender [said Paul], or have committed
any thing worthy of death, I refuse not to die: but if
there be none of these things whereof these accuse me,
no man may deliver me unto them. I appeal unto Caesar.*

Festus stalled around Jerusalem for ten days, then
went down to Caesarea, the Jews right with him. Once
more they made their stereotyped accusations against
the Apostle, once more he denied them; but this time
he asked to be heard by Caesar under his right as a
Roman citizen. Again the disgruntled Jews went back to
Jerusalem, and again Paul continued his semi-imprison-

ment at Caesarea. He didn't have to twist Festus' arm at all. Like Felix, Festus was glad for any "legal" reason to send the Jews home (verse 12).

vv. 13 and 14a

*And after certain days king Agrippa and Bernice came unto Caesarea to salute Festus. And when they had been there many days, Festus declared Paul's cause unto the king. . . .*

Paul, by then, was like a brier in Festus' finger. The governor told Agrippa the whole story of the Jews' accusations, of Paul's denial, and of his own hopefully wise handling of the case. "I asked this Christian, Paul, if he was willing to go back to Jerusalem to stand trial before the Jews themselves. He's a brilliant thinker. Immediately, he reminded me that although he was not unwilling to die, he was unwilling not to insist upon his legal rights as a Roman citizen. He appealed to Caesar. That's where things stand now. I'm simply holding the man. It's an interesting case—and an irritating one" (verses 14b through 21).

v. 22

*Then Agrippa said unto Festus, I would also hear the man myself. To morrow, said he, thou shalt hear him.*

Without a doubt, Festus was hoping for just this kind of response from his important guest. Maybe somehow, he thought, King Agrippa will come up with a helpful solution. He could send Paul to be heard before Caesar, but how would he, Festus, state the case (verses 25 through 27)?

v. 23

*And on the morrow, when Agrippa was come, and Bernice, with great pomp, and was entered into the place of hearing, with the chief captains, and principal men of the city, at Festus' commandment Paul was brought forth.*

How weary Paul must have been by now of being "brought forth" to be heard again on these nebulous, trumped-up charges!

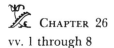 CHAPTER 26

vv. 1 through 8

*Then Agrippa said unto Paul, Thou art permitted to speak for thyself. Then Paul stretched forth the hand, and answered for himself: I think myself happy, king Agrippa, because I shall answer for myself this day before thee touching all the things whereof I am accused of the Jews. . . . My manner of life from my youth, which was at the first among mine own nation at Jerusalem, know all the Jews; Which knew me from the beginning, if they would testify, that after the most straitest sect of our religion I lived a Pharisee. And now I stand and am judged for the hope of the promise made of God unto our fathers. . . . Why should it be thought a thing incredible with you, that God should raise the* **dead?**

I see Paul standing with the characteristic out-stretched hand, determined once more to restate his case. His agile mind found a slightly new approach each time, and yet, to me, here, he almost bogged down —not in the sense of giving up; rather, in the sense of being suddenly swamped with the ludicrous facts of the case. His normally smooth flow of speech broke off, and he burst out with the question: "Why should it be thought incredible that God should raise the dead?" Why, indeed? He recouped, though, and plunged again into his personal witness to the trans-forming power of Jesus Christ.

vv. 9 through 11

*I verily thought with myself, that I ought to do many things contrary to the name of Jesus of Nazareth. Which thing I also did in Jerusalem: and many of the saints did I shut up in prison, having received authority from the chief priests; and when they were put to death, I gave my voice against them. And I punished them oft in every synagogue, and compelled them to blaspheme; and being exceedingly mad against them, I persecuted them even unto strange cities.*

I once read a brilliant treatise on Paul which argued that whatever his experience on the road to Damascus had been, it had surely left him warped and preoccupied with himself, a little mad. The basis for this argument was the above quotation from the Scriptures. Over and over, the author maintained, Paul reveled in boasting about his past sins. The conclusion stated that all persons who claim to have experienced an encounter with Jesus Christ begin to dwell unhealthily on their past sins. Some do. But I feel that most of those who do have been unhealthily influenced by other Christians attempting to spice up their meetings under the guise of letting God "use" the new converts' testimonies. After five years of telling the story of my own conversion to Jesus Christ in 1949, I banged down the lid. I have never told it again except once or twice when—to my own surprise—I found it tumbling out. This, I reasoned, must have been God's prompting. Unless Paul was in a predicament or before an audience where the telling of his own meeting with Christ on the Damascus road was relevant, he did not go over it again. The recounting (which he does very briefly here) of his past brutality against the followers of Jesus of Nazareth is an integral part of the story. He was not telling it again only to Festus. King Agrippa and his queen, Bernice, had not heard it before. Paul does repeat his past sins often in the New Testament, but always for a specific reason which even human intelligence alone would dictate.

vv. 12 through 15

*Whereupon as I went to Damascus with authority and commission from the chief priests, At midday, O king, I saw in the way a light from heaven, above the brightness of the sun, shining round about me and them which journeyed with me. And when we were all fallen to the earth, I heard a voice speaking unto me, and saying in the Hebrew tongue, Saul, Saul, why persecutest thou*

*me? it is hard for thee to kick against the pricks. And
I said, Who are thou, Lord? And he said, I am Jesus
whom thou persecutest.*

I can believe that when Paul spoke this name, King
Agrippa frowned and changed position in his chair,
and that Festus, nervous before his royal guest, began
to squirm in discomfort. But Paul would not be slowed
even now. There comes a particular inner-energizing
when one is telling of the actual meeting with the living Christ.

vv. 16 through 18

*But rise [the Lord said], and stand upon thy feet:
for I have appeared unto thee for this purpose, to make
thee a minister and a witness both of these things
which thou hast seen, and of those things in the which
I will appear unto thee; Delivering thee from the people, and from the Gentiles, unto whom now I send thee,
To open their eyes, and to turn them from darkness to
light, and from the power of Satan unto God, that they
may receive forgiveness of sins, and inheritance . . . by
faith that is in me.*

Paul must have sensed Festus' anxiety because he
continuously caught Agrippa's attention by using his
name again as he went resolutely on with his story:

vv. 19 through 23

*Whereupon, O king Agrippa, I was not disobedient
unto the heavenly vision: But shewed first unto them
of Damascus, and at Jerusalem, and throughout all the
coasts of Judaea, and then to the Gentiles, that they*

*should repent and turn to God, and do works meet for repentance. For these causes the Jews caught me in the temple, and went about to kill me. Having therefore obtained help of God, I continue unto this day, witnessing both to small and great, saying none other things than those which the prophets and Moses did say should come: That Christ should suffer, and that he should be the first that should rise from the dead, and should shew light unto the people, and to the Gentiles.*

Paul has been accused of boasting when he reiterated how much work he had done, mentioned the places to which he had traveled. I can understand why a superficial reading might cause one to think this, but after years of reading and rereading Paul's recorded journeys, I believe firmly that he mentioned these things only to impress his hearers with his own conviction that the "heavenly vision" on the road to Damascus was *real*—that his Lord was real, that Jesus of Nazareth *was* God, and that He did rise from the dead. I do not think Paul was being only dramatic or self aggrandizing. He stood before Agrippa a convinced man. If he had spoken otherwise, he would have compromised his own integrity. I have wondered if Paul was really finished with what he had to say that day as he stood before Agrippa and Festus. We shall never know, because Festus had heard enough:

v. 24

*And as he thus spake for himself, Festus said with a loud voice, Paul, thou art beside thyself; much learning doth make thee mad.*

Paul had spoken more of Jesus this time than on his first defense before Festus. It was too much for Festus. He lost his poise and shouted at Paul that he was insane. There are those who contend that Festus was also "under conviction" before God. It seems more plausible that he just didn't want to be embarrassed before Agrippa by having Paul go into too much personal detail. Festus' attitude is neither right nor wrong. It is simply pagan. He is more aware of royal proprieties and his position as governor than he is of spiritual truths.

vv. 25 through 27

*But he [Paul] said, I am not mad, most noble Festus; but speak forth the words of truth and soberness. For the king knoweth of these things, before whom also I speak freely: for I am persuaded that none of these things are hidden from him; for this thing was not done in a corner.*

Paul knew that Agrippa had had Jewish upbringing and was aware of the promise of the Lord God. He had now decided to be direct with the king in his next statement.

v. 27

*King Agrippa, believest thou the prophets? I know that thou believest.*

Paul may have smiled a little when he answered his own question. The continuity between the Old and the New Testament messages was so clear to Paul that perhaps he even hoped for a moment it had been clarified for Agrippa too.

v. 28

*Then Agrippa said unto Paul, Almost thou persuadest me to be a Christian.*

This short reply from the king has been, and still is, a controversial verse. I fail to see any reason for actual controversy here, but I do see how it can be interpreted in two ways. The problem obviously is in the translation. The King James Version used here easily indicates that Agrippa was on the verge of believing in Jesus Christ as the promised Messiah, but the newer, more accurate translations do not read this way at all. Only Phillips tilts in the direction of Agrippa's seriousness about Paul's message: " 'Much more of this, Paul,' returned Agrippa, 'and you will be making me a Christian!' " In *Good News for Modern Man*, the American Bible Society's highly contemporary translation, verse 28 is phrased this way: "Agrippa said to Paul, 'In this short time you think you will make me a Christian?' " And in *The Amplified Bible:* "Then Agrippa said to Paul, You think it a small task to make a Christian of me—just off hand to induce me with little ado and persuasion, at very short notice." Most of the so-called controversy stems from human curiosity. I tend to believe that Agrippa was more involved in his kingly position and riches than in eternal verities, and so I find the phrasing in *Good News for Modern Man* more acceptable.

v. 29

*And Paul said, I would to God, that not only thou, but also all that hear me this day, were both almost, and altogether such as I am, except these bonds.*

Paul may also have smiled a little here, as one does when it is evident that the gift of truth has been overlooked. I don't think he smiled from a superior spiritual place; rather, sadly, seeing as he did that his "riches in Christ" far outshone all their worldly pomp and wealth.

vv. 30 through 32

*And when he had thus spoken, the king rose up, and the governor, and Bernice, and they that sat with them: And when they were gone aside, they talked between themselves, saying, This man doeth nothing worthy of death or of bonds. Then said Agrippa unto Festus, This man might have been set at liberty, if he had not appealed unto Caesar.*

Paul has been pronounced innocent, but "aside" only among Festus, Agrippa, Bernice and their official circle. The verdict did not free Paul. He had appealed to Caesar and he would be sent to Rome. God had promised that his loyal disciple would witness in Rome.

Paul was on his way at last. Nowhere in the New Testament are the basic premises of Christianity more clearly explained than in Paul's words before Agrippa: At the very heart of the Christian faith is the *fact* of the resurrected Lord, Jesus Christ; and through him, and him only, comes forgiveness—both for Jews and Gentiles. The "middle wall of partition" is knocked down here once and for all. Paul did not lose. He would go on to Rome in chains, but he had fulfilled his mission. He had fulfilled the purpose of the Christ who met him on the road to Damascus: Before Agrippa and Festus, Paul was a witness to the Lord who *was* Paul's very life. The rest he could leave up to God. It is interesting that Paul did not press his argument with Agrippa. The great Apostle had learned the all-important lesson that no man, even Paul, ever needs to "play God."

 CHAPTER 27

v. 1

> *And when it was determined that we should sail into Italy, they delivered Paul and certain other prisoners unto one named Julius, a centurion of Augustus' band.*

Luke had evidently used the more than two years' imprisonment of Paul in Caesarea to gather material for his Gospel. Now he has rejoined his hero, Paul, and will sail with him to Rome. The narrative resumes in the first person, *we.*

vv. 2 and 3

*And entering into a ship of Adramyttium, we launched, meaning to sail by the coasts of Asia; one Aristarchus, a Macedonian of Thessalonica, being with us. And the next day we touched at Sidon. And Julius courteously entreated Paul, and gave him liberty to go unto his friends to refresh himself.*

There was no boat direct to Rome, so Paul and his guard, Captain Julius; Luke; Aristarchus, another friend of Paul's; and the other prisoners also going to Rome embarked on a ship heading toward Myra, where they hoped to make a further connection (verse 5). Luke's attention to Paul is touching. The "beloved physician" seems always genuinely pleased when some courtesy is shown Paul. In Sidon, Captain Julius, evidently an admirer of the Apostle, had permitted him to spend some time ashore with the Christians there "to refresh himself."

vv. 9 and 10

*Now when much time was spent, and when sailing was now dangerous, because the fast was now already past, Paul admonished them, And said unto them, Sirs, I perceive that this voyage will be with hurt and much damage, not only of the lading and ship, but also of our lives.*

I don't think Paul was soothsaying here. He simply knew that navigation was dependent on the winds and

always difficult after September—practically impossible
in November. It was already early October; the fast
of the Day of Atonement was past. They had managed
to board a ship (most likely a grain ship) at Myra, but
Paul's common sense caused him to warn them of the
dangers ahead. Captain Julius admired Paul, but he
chose to take the advice of the ship's master, who
wanted more than anything else to get his cargo out
of that unfit harbor before winter set in (verse 11).

vv. 13 through 17

*And when the south wind blew softly, supposing that
they had obtained their purpose, loosing thence, they
sailed close by Crete. But not long after there arose
against it a tempestuous wind, called Euroclydon [a
northeaster]. And when the ship was caught, and could
not bear up into the wind, we let her drive. And running under a certain island which is called Clauda, we
had much work to come by the boat: Which when they
had taken up, they used helps, undergirding the ship;
and, fearing lest they should fall into the quicksands,
strake sail, and so were driven.*

At first, Paul seemed to have been overly cautious.
A soft, south wind blew and, since most of the men
preferred the dangers of a voyage to the unsafe harbor
at Myra as a winter haven, they sailed—almost straight
into a gigantic windstorm. In an effort to make the
ship's wooden lifeboat secure, they "undergirded" it;
i.e., they bound the boat round and round with strong
cables so that the timbers would not break apart. Fear-

ing the sandbanks off the coast of Libya, they lowered the sail and let the ship be carried by the wind.

vv. 18 through 19

*And we being exceedingly tossed with a tempest, the next day they lightened the ship; And the third day we cast out with our own hands the tackling of the ship.*

Now the storm was so severe that even the prisoners, Paul and the others, and Luke and Aristarchus were put to work to lighten the ship. What is referred to as "tackling" was probably all the superfluous equipment aboard.

v. 20

*And when neither sun nor stars in many days appeared, and no small tempest lay on us, all hope that we should be saved was then taken away.*

Day after day the sky hung above them—too dark for stars, even too dark to see the sun—and "all hope" vanished. Luke does not say that Paul alone believed they would be saved. He simply wrote: "All hope that we should be saved was then taken away." After all, they had no compasses; they steered by the stars. Even Paul's hope was gone. I am better able to lay hold of Paul's high moments when I remember his times of humanity such as this. He was not a super-Christian; he was simply a human being filled with the life of God.

vv. 21 through 26

*But after long abstinence Paul stood forth in the midst of them, and said, Sirs, ye should have hearkened unto me, and not have loosed from Crete, and to have gained this harm and loss. And now I exhort you to be of good cheer: for there shall be no loss of any man's life among you, but of the ship. For there stood by me this night the angel of God, whose I am, and whom I serve, Saying, Fear not, Paul; thou must be brought before Caesar: and, lo, God hath given thee all them that sail with thee. Wherefore, sirs, be of good cheer: for I believe God, that it shall be even as it was told me. Howbeit we must be cast upon a certain island.*

Paul, still utterly human, could not resist an "I told you so," but with great certainty he told the men what God had shown him of their fate. Luke doesn't say whether or not anyone believed Paul; he just goes right on with his dramatic narrative, taking care to describe even the smallest details. Obviously, this storm at sea was the most traumatic event of Luke's life.

vv. 27 through 29

*But when the fourteenth night was come, as we were driven up and down in Adria [the Mediterranean waters], about midnight the shipmen deemed that they drew near to some country; And sounded, and found it twenty fathoms [120 feet]: and when they had gone a little further, they sounded again, and found it fifteen fathoms [90 feet]. Then fearing lest we should have fallen upon rocks, they cast four anchors out of the stern, and wished for the day.*

Luke does not say that Paul was now in command
of the ship, but the actions of the shipmen showed
that at least they had listened when Paul had declared
that they would go aground on an island. Normally
anchors are dropped from the prow of a ship, but in
this case they were eager to keep her headed toward
the shore, just in case Paul was right.

vv. 30 through 32

*And as the shipmen were about to flee out of the ship,
when they had let down the boat into the sea, under
colour as though they would have cast anchors out of
the foreship, Paul said to the centurion and to the soldiers, Except these abide in the ship, ye cannot be saved.
Then the soldiers cut off the ropes of the boat, and let
her fall off.*

Evidently some of the men did not believe Paul, so
great was their fright. At least, under cover of the
night, they attempted to get away in the lifeboat. But
when Paul insisted to his friend, Captain Julius, that
only those who stayed on the ship would be saved,
any doubt that Paul was theoretically in charge was
gone. The men were ordered to cut the ropes and let
the boat fall into the water. The die was cast. They
would follow Paul's orders.

vv. 33 and 34

*And while the day was coming on, Paul besought
them all to take meat, saying, This day is the fourteenth
day that ye have tarried and continued fasting, having*

*taken nothing. Wherefore I pray you to take some meat:
for this is for your health: for there shall not an hair
fall from the head of any of you.*

Paul was not a weirdo. No matter how strange his
message sounded to the pagan ears of Felix and Festus,
as with any Christian centered down in Jesus Christ,
Paul was practical. He had had his word from the Lord
about their safety, but his intelligence told him to urge
these starving, frightened men to break their fast and
eat. "This is for your health," he said. God is interested
in our health because it is irrevocably tied up with our
spiritual lives. They are one to Christ because he is a
realist, and no one knows better than he that "in the
beginning" a whole person was created.

vv. 35 through 38

*And when he had thus spoken, he took bread, and
gave thanks to God in presence of them all: and when
he had broken it, he began to eat. Then were they all
of good cheer, and they also took some meat. And we
were in all in the ship two hundred threescore and six-
teen souls [276 people]. And when they had eaten
enough, they lightened the ship, and cast out the wheat
into the sea.*

To Paul there was no sacred and no secular. All of
life was "of a piece" in God. He gave orders of a practical nature and prayed in one motion, then ate first
to show the men that he held no more fears for his

own life. It worked. They all ate, and "they were all of good cheer" suddenly.

vv. 39 through 44

*And when it was day, they knew not the land: but they discovered a certain creek with a shore, into the which they were minded, if it were possible, to thrust in the ship. And when they had taken up the anchors, they committed themselves unto the sea, and loosed the rudder bands, and hoised up the mainsail to the wind, and made toward shore. And falling into a place where two seas met, they ran the ship aground; and the forepart stuck fast, and remained unmoveable, but the hinder part was broken with the violence of the waves. And the soldiers' counsel was to kill the prisoners, lest any of them should swim out, and escape. But the centurion, willing to save Paul, kept them from their purpose; and commanded that they which could swim should cast themselves first into the sea, and get to land: And the rest, some on boards, and some on broken pieces of the ship. And so it came to pass, that they escaped all safe to land.*

I wish Luke, who had been so detailed up to now, had told us how Paul got to land; how Luke reached shore, too, and the kind centurion, and Aristarchus. At any rate, they all made it. God's promise to Paul held. And it is certainly well for us to note that Paul had to do his part too in bringing that promise to fulfillment. There was no celestial magic wand-waving performed here. God made no supernatural miracle of it. He simply told Paul that they would make it—and they did. He spared his beloved disciple no hard knocks in the process. The Almighty did not reach down and whisk Paul to shore just because he "had fought the good fight." Paul swam or splashed his way to the beach on a broken bit of ship, just like the others. Neither Paul nor God was vindicated. Neither needed to be. I believe Luke gave so much space to the story of the shipwreck because it ran so much the way most of life runs. Good advice ignored, stormy seas, frail ships, lost hope, prayer, practical action, faith, struggle—and with God, eventually the shore.

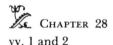 CHAPTER 28

vv. 1 and 2

*And when they were escaped, then they knew that the island was called Melita [Malta]. And the barbarous people shewed us no little kindness: for they kindled a fire, and received us every one, because of the present rain, and because of the cold.*

These people of the island of Melita were not "barbarians" in the sense that we use the word. "Barbarians" as Luke uses it here is merely the Greek word for all people who did not speak Greek. These islanders were not only kind and hospitable; they were cultivated and prosperous. The whole rescue operation of Melita must have been welcomed by Paul. He was overjoyed to see friendly faces and strong arms to pull them out of the icy winter sea; but more than that, Paul must have reveled in being treated like a free man again. Standing on the beach of Malta in the pouring, cold rain, Paul, I feel sure, in spite of his physical discomfort, could not help contrasting the kindness of these strange pagans with the vindictiveness of the Jews and the trickery of the Romans who had kept him in chains. So far as we know, there were no believers on Melita, but God was there in their kindness to the shipwrecked men.

vv. 3 and 4

*And when Paul had gathered a bundle of sticks, and laid them on the fire, there came a viper out of the heat, and fastened on his hand. And when the barbarians saw the venomous beast hang on his hand, they said among themselves, No doubt this man is a murderer, whom, though he hath escaped the sea, yet vengeance suffereth not to live.*

In the confusion of the rescue from the sea, no one had noticed Paul among the crowd until, as he worked along with the others, a snake fastened onto his hand as he threw a bundle of sticks on the hastily built fire. Even the pagan mind has a sense of right and wrong and believes in some manner of punishment for wrong, so Luke evidently overheard one of the islanders speculate that Paul must be a murderer getting his just due in spite of the rescue from the storm. They knew that the snake was deadly. Paul would surely die.

vv. 5 and 6

*And he shook off the beast into the fire, and felt no harm. Howbeit they looked when he should have swollen, or fallen down dead suddenly: but after they had looked a great while, and saw no harm come to him, they changed their minds, and said that he was a god.*

I do not see this startling episode as an indication that God's people are cosmic pets who will be protected from deadly vipers. In my home state of West Virginia, back in the mountains, are religious cults called "snake handlers," who use this incident on the beach at Melita as their basic doctrine. True, Jesus said that his disciples "should take up serpents," but he spoke often in colorful Eastern metaphors; and at this point on my journey I am trying to understand the Scriptures by the light of what I have come to understand about the nature of Jesus Christ. He, as Dr. E. Stanley Jones says, "was all sanctity, but he was also all sanity." I live in snake country now, on an island—my house surrounded by woods and marsh—but I see no sanity in counting on divine protection, and so I have learned to enjoy the woods with one eye on the ground. We should not attempt any sort of explanation as to why God did this for Paul. He had a reason, and all manner of speculation is possible. For one thing, a sudden act of this kind focused attention on Paul. God had promised Paul he would witness in Rome, and they weren't there yet. What is relevant is what happens next, and none of it could have happened if Paul had lain on the sand dead from snakebite.

v. 7

*In the same quarters were possessions of the chief man of the island, whose name was Publius; who received us, and lodged us three days courteously.*

Paul was "somebody" now—a "god," the people said—and so he and Luke and Aristarchus were entertained "courteously" at the home of the island's most important official.

vv. 8 through 10

*And it came to pass, that the father of Publius lay sick of a fever and of a bloody flux: to whom Paul entered in, and prayed, and laid his hands on him, and healed him. So when this was done, others also, which had diseases in the island, came, and were healed: Who also honoured us with many honours; and when we departed, they laded us with such things as were necessary.*

God seldom has just one simple purpose in what he does. If Paul had died, none of these people would have been healed, none of them would have heard the Gospel of Christ—and we may be sure they did, even though Luke does not mention it. For Paul "to live was Christ"; he could no more have healed those people without telling them about the Healer than he could have lived without breathing. This is a lovely example

not only of the rhythmic two-way motion of the kingdom of love, but of God's constant concern with the
total person. Paul prayed for the Maltese and they sup-
plied his needs. Nothing ever works just one way in the
kingdom of love, and love abounded on Melita for the
three months Paul and his party lived there.

vv. 11 through 14

*And after three months we departed in a ship of
Alexandria, which had wintered in the isle, whose sign
was Castor and Pollux. And landing at Syracuse, we
tarried there three days. And from thence we fetched
a compass, and came to Rhegium: and after one day the
south wind blew, and we came the next day to Puteoli:
Where we found brethren, and were desired to tarry
with them seven days: and so we went toward Rome.*

Another Greek grain ship had wintered at friendly
Melita, and Paul and his party secured passage to leave
as soon as winter was over and navigation was again
possible. Luke, the physician, seems to be quite carried
away with ships and winds and the problems of sailing;
he is still being rather detailed about these things.
Quite probably, Luke had never sailed so much on the
high seas before, and he relished it.

Paul had lived for a long time with the conviction
that he would eventually die a martyr's death in Rome.
"Yea, and if I be offered upon the sacrifice and service
of your faith, I joy, and rejoice with you all." He had
already written this in his letter to the church at
Philippi. After the troubled years, death could have

been no surprise to the Apostle, and he was on his way to Rome—joyfully, because God was sending him. Luke mentions only one stop with "the brethren," but he says "and so we went toward Rome." There must have been other meetings along the way to encourage and warm Paul's heart.

v. 15

*And from thence, when the brethren heard of us, they came to meet us as far as Appii forum, and The three taverns: whom when Paul saw, he thanked God, and took courage.*

It had been a long time—more than three years— since Paul wrote his letter to the Roman Christians telling them of his desire to visit them. "For God is my witness, whom I serve with my spirit in the gospel of his Son, that without ceasing I make mention of you always in my prayers; Making request, if by any means now at length I might have a prosperous journey by the will of God to come unto you. For I long to see you, that I may impart unto you some spiritual gift, to the end ye may be established: That is, that I may be comforted together with you by the mutual faith both of you and me. Now I would not have you ignorant, brethren, that oftentimes I purposed to come unto you, (but was let hitherto,) that I might have some fruit among you also, even as among other Gentiles." The long wait was ended at last, and Paul joyfully embraced one group after another of the Roman Christians, who couldn't wait for him to reach them, but hurried out to greet him with open arms and hearts. After what he had been through, Paul needed them as much as they needed him.

v. 16

*And when we came to Rome, the centurion delivered the prisoners to the captain of the guard: but Paul was suffered to dwell by himself with a soldier that kept him.*

Paul was innocent of the Jews' charges, and yet there was the legal technicality of his appearance before Caesar still ahead. He was not free, in spite of the private quarters where he was permitted to live. He was still in bonds, with a soldier to guard him.

vv. 17 through 20

*And it came to pass, that after three days Paul called the chief of the Jews together: and when they were come together, he said unto them, Men and brethren, though I have committed nothing against the people, or customs of our fathers, yet was I delivered prisoner from Jerusalem into the hands of the Romans. Who, when they had examined me, would have let me go, because there was no cause of death in me. But when the Jews spake against it, I was constrained to appeal unto Caesar; not that I had ought to accuse my nation of. For this cause therefore have I called for you, to see you, and to speak with you: because that for the hope of Israel I am bound with this chain.*

Paul had scarcely arrived in Rome before he called the Jews to him. With all his mind and heart Paul's faith was in Jesus, the Messiah, but he remained a Jew. Three days after he reached Rome, found a rented house and settled in, he invited the Roman Jews to visit him and once more poured out his great heart and the story of his persecution by the Jerusalem rulers. He was still in chains, not free to go to them at the synagogue, but he had to see them—had to let them hear from his own lips what had really happened.

vv. 21 and 22

*And they said unto him, We neither received letters out of Judaea concerning thee, neither any of the brethren that came shewed or spake any harm of thee. But we desire to hear of thee what thou thinkest: for as concerning this sect, know that everywhere it is spoken against.*

Paul's heart must have leapt up. They had heard no ill of him. He could be hopeful again—hopeful of freedom, perhaps, on the charges but, more than that, hopeful that, by some means, he might be able to help these Jews see that their Messiah had come in Jesus Christ. At least they professed interest in finding out what Paul believed. They would give him a fair hearing. I can almost *feel* his hope.

vv. 23 and 24

*And when they had appointed him a day, there came many to him into his lodging; to whom he expounded and testified the kingdom of God, persuading them concerning Jesus, both out of the law of Moses, and out of*

*the prophets, from morning till evening. And some
believed the things which were spoken, and some believed not.*

From morning until evening Paul poured out his
heart and his knowledge to these men, using the Scriptures with which they were all familiar to prove that
God had already sent the promised Messiah in Jesus
of Nazareth. "And some believed . . . and some believed
not." Paul's audience that day in his little rented house
was like any church audience today—some believe and
some do not. But being Paul, he could not be satisfied
with half measures. To his Jewish mind, it was all so
clear—so real, so irrefutable. In spite of their maltreatment of him, Paul still seemed to expect more
spiritual perception, more definite recognition of the
truth from his fellow Jews. Some apparently did believe
him, but when they left his house that day they were
all arguing (verse 25a).

vv. 25 through 27

*And when they agreed not among themselves, they
departed, after that Paul had spoken one word, Well
spake the Holy Ghost by Esaias the prophet unto our
fathers, Saying, Go unto this people, and say, Hearing
ye shall hear, and shall not understand; and seeing ye
shall see, and not perceive: For the heart of this people
is waxed gross, and their ears are dull of hearing, and
their eyes have they closed; lest they should see with
their eyes, and hear with their ears, and understand with
their heart, and should be converted, and I should heal
them.*

As the men began to leave Paul's house arguing among themselves, he stopped them with one more word from Isaiah. I see in this last desperate attempt no rancor on Paul's part—disappointment, yes, but to me it is a final effort to reach them through Isaiah, their own prophet, who had accurately described the scene in Paul's house that day.

vv. 28 and 29

*Be it known therefore unto you, that the salvation of God is sent unto the Gentiles, and that they will hear it. And when he had said these words, the Jews departed, and had great reasoning among themselves.*

Paul had done all he knew to do to reach his brothers. He may have sat down at this point with a long, heavy sigh. "I must tell you then, that God's message is going to be given to the Gentiles. They will listen!" He had done all he knew how, and his hopes for most of his brothers faded as he watched them walk away from his house, arguing as though they had heard little more than another philosophical premise.

vv. 30 and 31

*And Paul dwelt two whole years in his own hired house, and received all that came in unto him, Preaching the kingdom of God, and teaching those things which concern the Lord Jesus Christ, with all confidence, no man forbidding him.*

Luke seems to have ended this gripping story of Paul rather abruptly. As I pointed out earlier, his account of the Acts of the Apostles is not a biography of Paul. It is, as J. B. Phillips wrote, "Some acts of some apostles." It is quite probable that, when Paul seemed settled down in Rome to wait for his appearance before Caesar, Luke returned home to work on his Gospel account. Paul was content because he was not forbidden to preach Jesus Christ, the risen Lord, and long ago he had learned to be content in chains. This man, Paul, was the bond servant of Jesus Christ—iron chains could not bind him—and I can imagine that Paul urged Luke to put the finishing touches on his Gospel. Nothing would have pleased the great Apostle more than to have his beloved friend hard at work on the story of Jesus of Nazareth, the Son of God.

In two years Paul would be beheaded by the young Caesar, and Luke's Gospel would be available to us so that we, too, could be sure that Paul was right when he said that Jesus is "the Son of God with power, according to the spirit of holiness, by the resurrection from the dead. . . . and that in him should all fullness dwell."

Printed in the USA
CPSIA information can be obtained
at www.ICGtesting.com
JSHW082345140824
68134JS00020B/1901